Internet
New York

Internet
New York

Hayden
Books

Internet New York

©1994 Hayden Books

All rights reserved. Printed in the United States of America. No part of this book may be used or reproduced in any form or by any means, or stored in a database or retrieval system, without prior written permission of the publisher except in the case of brief quotations embodied in critical articles and reviews. Making copies of any part of this book for any purpose other than your own personal use is a violation of United States copyright laws. For information, address Hayden Books, 201 W. 103rd Street, Indianapolis, IN, 46290.

Library of Congress Catalog No.: 94-77935

ISBN: 1-56830-039-5

This book is sold as is, without warranty of any kind, either express or implied. While every precaution has been taken in the preparation of this book, the publisher and authors assume no responsibility for errors or omissions. Neither is any liability assumed for damages resulting from the use of the information or instructions contained herein. It is further stated that the publisher and author are not responsible for any damage or loss to your data or your equipment that results directly or indirectly from your use of this book.

96   95   4   3   2

Interpretation of the printing code: the rightmost double-digit number is the year of the book's printing; the rightmost single-digit number the number of the book's printing. For example, a printing code of 94-1 shows that the first printing of the book occurred in 1994.

Trademark Acknowledgments: All products mentioned in this book are either trademarks of the companies referenced in this book, registered trademarks of the companies referenced in this book, or neither. We strongly advise that you investigate a particular product's name thoroughly before you use the name as your own.

The Hayden Books Team

Contributors

Part I   Brad Miser, Adam Engst

Part II   David Blumenstein, Brian Gill

Part III Corwin Low

Part IV   Adam Engst

(Part IV is condensed from *Internet Starter Kit for Macintosh, 2nd Edition* by Adam Engst, Hayden Books, 1994. Condensed by Brian Gill.)

Publisher
David Rogelberg

Managing Editor
Karen Whitehouse

Development Editor
Brad Miser

Copy/Production Editor
Brian Gill

Cover Designer
Jay Corpus

Interior Designer
Fred Bower

Production Team
Gary Adair, Dan Caparo, Brad Chinn, Kim Cofer, David Dean, Lisa Daugherty, Jennifer Eberhardt, David Garratt, Erika Millen, Beth Rago, Bobbi Satterfield, Karen Walsh, Robert Wolf

Indexers
Rebecca Mayfield, Bront Davis

Composed in 1Stone Serif and MCPdigital

To Our Readers

Dear Friend,

Thank you on behalf of everyone at Hayden Books for choosing *Internet New York* to enable you to discover some of the regional resources the Internet offers. One of the reasons that the Internet is so powerful is that it is both global and local at the same time. Without the right guide, finding the local resources can sometimes be difficult and time consuming. We hope that this book enables you to use the Internet to explore your corner of the globe easily and enjoyably.

What you think of this book is important to our ability to better serve you in the future. If you have any comments, no matter how great or small, we'd appreciate you taking the time to send us email or a note by snail mail. Of course, we'd love to hear your book ideas.

Sincerely yours,

Publisher, Hayden Books and Adobe Press

You can reach Hayden Books at the following:

Hayden Books
201 West 103rd Street
Indianapolis, IN 46290
(800) 428-5331 voice
(800) 448-3804 fax

Email addresses:

America Online:	Hayden Bks
CompuServe:	76350,3014
Internet:	hayden@hayden.com

Contents at a Glance

Part I	**Welcome to Internet New York**	**3**
	What the Regional Guide Is	4
	What the Regional Guide Is Not	5
	Using the Regional Guide	5
Part II	**New York Guide**	**9**
	The Sites	10
Part III	**Internet Providers**	**45**
	New York Area Providers	47
	National Providers	51
Part IV	**Internet Overview**	**57**
	What is the Internet?	58
	What Can You Do on the Internet?	61
	How Did the Internet Get Here?	72
Index		**95**

Internet New York

Table of Contents

Part I Welcome to Internet New York — 3
    What the Regional Guide Is — 4
    What the Regional Guide Is Not — 5
    Using the Regional Guide — 5

Part II New York Guide — 9
    The Sites — 10

Part III Internet Providers — 45
    New York Area Providers — 47
    National Providers — 51

Part IV Internet Overview — 57
    What is the Internet? — 58
    What Can You Do on the Internet? — 61
        Electronic Mail — 62
        Usenet News — 64
        Telnet — 65
        File Transfer Protocol (FTP) — 65
        Archie — 66
        WAIS — 68
        Gopher — 69
        World-Wide Web — 71
        There is More — 72
    How Did the Internet Get Here? — 72
        Cold War Network — 72
        Gateways — 76
        Usenet — 77
        BITNET — 79
        NSFNET — 80
        NREN — 81
        Who Pays? — 82
        Politics — 86
        The Future — 88

Index — 95

XI

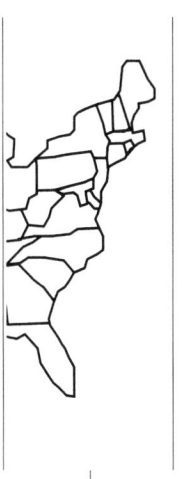

Part I

Welcome to Internet New York

Internet New York

When people talk about the Internet, they usually talk about the fact that it spans the globe and connects millions of people in a variety of countries. And this is true. But what many people don't realize is that the Internet is also local. By that I mean that there are many resources on the net that are devoted to your corner of the world—New York.

There are newsgroups devoted to the discussion of New York politics, sports teams, and social issues. You can access local city and state government services. New York area universities maintain World-Wide Web sites and provide research capabilities for you to use. You can read the opinions of fellow New Yorkers regarding entertainment and restaurants. And much more.

That's what this book is about: helping you use the power of the global Internet to interact with fellow New Yorkers. Find out what is going on locally, learn about the hot spots (and cold spots) of the city, and meet people in New York who share your interests.

What the Regional Guide Is

Internet New York has four parts; each provides you with specific information to help you understand and use the "local" Internet.

Part I explains how this guide is organized and how you might want to use it.

Part II provides a listing of Internet sites and resources that are devoted to the New York area. You'll find the information that you need to connect to the site, a description of it, and a review to help you decide whether to explore the site or not.

Part III lists Internet providers to help you find a provider that gives you the access you want at a cost you can afford. You'll find everything you need to contact these companies, as well as information on the services each provider offers. Even if you already have a provider, you should review this list to see if there is one that better suits your needs.

Part IV provides you with an overview of the Internet. It consists of three sections that describe what the Internet is, what you can do on it, and a brief history so that you will understand it a little better.

What the Regional Guide Is Not

You should know that this book will not give you the details of how to connect to the Internet. Nor does it describe the step-by-step procedures of getting to a certain site. If you need to connect to the net or learn how to use Internet software, you should buy and read *Internet Starter Kit for Macintosh* or *Internet Starter Kit for Windows* (both Hayden Books, 1994).

The specific techniques for connecting to and using the Internet are computer-specific—those details are beyond the scope of this guide. The purpose here is to provide information on the Internet that is specific to New York.

Using the Regional Guide

Before we get to the information for your region, I want to explain *URLs*, or Uniform Resource Locators. These constitute the most common and efficient methods of telling people about resources available via FTP, the World-Wide Web, and other Internet services.

A URL, quite simply, is a method of uniquely specifying the location of a resource on the Internet. Depending on how you break it down, there are three main pieces you must know in order to retrieve any given resource. First, you have to know how to access the resource, be it on FTP, Gopher, or the World-Wide Web. Second, you must know the machine on which the resource lives. Finally, you must know the full pathname to the information you want.

> **note** Uniform Resource Locators have become so popular, the Library of Congress has added a subfield for them when it catalogs electronic resources.

This description is somewhat of an oversimplification, because the subject of URLs is extremely complex. The point I want to make is simply that URLs are an attempt to provide a consistent way to reference objects on the Internet. I say "objects" because you can specify URLs for email addresses, Telnet sessions, and stranger things that may not even seem like "objects."

Table I.1 shows the main URL types that you're likely to see.

Table I.1
Common URL Types

Name	Internet Protocol
ftp	File Transfer Protocol
gopher	Gopher protocol
http	HyperText Transfer Protocol (World-Wide Web)
wais	Wide Area Information Server

Part I

If you see a URL that starts with **ftp**, you know that the file specified in the rest of the URL is available via FTP. If the URL starts with **gopher**, use a Gopher client. If it starts with **http**, use a web browser. And, finally, if a URL starts with **wais**, you can use a WAIS browser to access the resource.

After the URL is a colon (:) and two slashes (//). These separate the type from the second part of common URLs. This second part is the name of the machine that contains the information you're seeking.

The last part of the URL is the path to the directory of the file you're looking for. This is separated from the machine name by a slash (/). When used with WAIS or various other protocols that don't simply point at files, the path may specify other types of information. You may not have to specify the path with some URLs, such as FTP or Gopher URLs, if you're only connecting to the top level of the site.

So, when you see an address that begins with something like **http://**, you should know to use a web browser to go to the site. If it begins with **ftp://**, you use an FTP client and enter the entire address. Simple enough, eh?

Some addresses in part II won't have a URL. If not, you can tell how to access that item by looking at the Type of Service the item uses. For example, if an item is **sample.news.com** and the Type of Service is newsgroup, you know that you need to use a news reader to receive the newsgroup. It's really not hard—trust me on this.

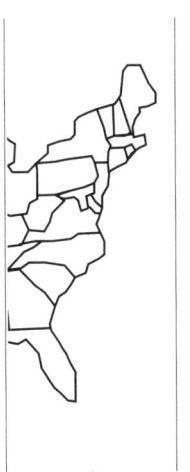

Part II

New York Guide

Internet New York

To list every site in the New York area would have been impossible, so what we tried to do is pick the best and most stable sites. By the time this book was printed, some of these may have disappeared, and a few new sites were probably added. So don't be too surprised if you type in an address and your computer tells you that the site does not exist. However, most will work just fine.

If this bothers you, there are places you can receive new information. For the best up-to-the minute information, we recommend Stanford University's "Yahoo—A Guide to the WWW" server. OK, the name isn't so hot, but the site is excellent. It contains many of the entries we have listed here, and is an excellent tool for the web and more.

Spend some time exploring this site. Its address is:

`http://akebono.stanford.edu/yahoo/`

However, we strongly urge you not to use this server too often. Too much traffic ties up the server and those who really need it are left in the dark. You already have the addresses of many of the resources that this server offers in your hands right now. You should use the server every so often, and maybe pencil a few new addresses in this book.

The Sites

The following information is listed in alphabetical order by address. So if you're looking for a web site look for `http:`, if your looking for a New York newsgroup, look for `ny` or `nyc`, and so on. Each entry contains an address, the type of service the site offers (World-Wide Web, FTP, and so on), the categories to which the service relates (politics, discussion, and so forth), and a brief description and review of the site. Some sites have special or alternate access information listed following the review.

alt.culture.ny-upstate

Type of Service   Newsgroup

Category   Local Information

Description   New York state, above Westchester

Review

There's more to New York than just the five boroughs of NYC. This newsgroup exists to discuss all things not New York City. After all, New York state attracts record numbers of vacationers to its statewide parks and recreational areas. The finger lake region has long been known for its wine production. SUNY, the State University system, is one of the strongest academic systems in the United States. And don't forget cities like Buffalo, Syracuse, Rochester, and so on.

Discussion in this newsgroup is generally friendly conversation among residents or former residents of upstate New York. At press time, discussions revolved around hockey, a debate whether to call a carbonated drink soda or pop, and a political debate/flame war. Another conversation continued among some New Yorkers that pretty much sums up the upstate New Yorker attitude:

"I had a funny experience when driving cross-country with friends back in '86. We pulled into a rest stop in Mississippi, or some other ungodly place, and this greasy green-toother pumping gas next to me says, "Where you fruuuum?"

"New York", I said politely, looking down at my license plate.

"Ever been mugged?"
I'm from a small town north of Albany. Cows don't mug.
"Yeah, a few times," I said.

alt.sports.baseball.ny-mets

Type of Service	Newsgroup
Category	Sports
Description	New York Mets baseball talk

Review

It's not like New Yorkers don't have enough outlets to dissect the ups and downs of the Amazings, but this newsgroup lets transplanted fans share in the joy of victory ('69 and '86) and the agony of defeat (all other seasons).
At the end of 1994, with the strike and all, discussions were kept to a minimum, but there is still a lot to talk about. Discussions surrounded "trades that made you cry" and finding the Mets a new catcher.

alt.sports.baseball.ny-yankees

Type of Service	Newsgroup
Category	Sports
Description	New York Yankees baseball talk

Review

At press time, discussions surrounded the '95 team, injuries, who should have received the Cy Young award, and a very popular tally of all-time favorite Yankees. Mickey Mantle had the majority of first place votes; Babe Ruth and Don Mattingly were in the race for second.

alt.sports.basketball.pro.ny-knicks

Type of Service	Newsgroup
Category	Sports
Description	New York Knicks basketball

Review

Rounded discussion about New York Knicks basketball. Topics vary here more than in most newsgroups. Discussion participants seem to enjoy debating and commenting on every aspect of the game.

alt.sports.football.pro.ny-giants

Type of Service	Newsgroup
Category	Sports
Description	New York Giants football

Review

Granted, they play in the Meadowlands, and that's in New Jersey. But the Jints will always be a part of New York whether they play in Yankee Stadium, Shea Stadium, or... New Jersey. This newsgroup centers around fans' discussions and flames from fans of opposing teams. Game reviews and previews abound. Everybody seems to know what went wrong and what the team should do next. It seems that many armchair quarterbacks have converted to keyboard quarterbacks.

alt.sports.football.pro.ny-jets

Type of Service	Newsgroup

Internet New York

Category	Sports
Description	New York Jets football

Review

Same as `alt.sports.football.pro.ny-giants`, only different.

alt.sports.football.pro.buf-bills

Type of Service	Newsgroup
Category	Sports
Description	Buffalo Bills football

Review

NOT. This site doesn't exist. The Bills don't have a newsgroup. I'd hide if my team lost that many Super Bowls in a row, too. I guess the only thing they have to discuss is... hiring Jimmy Johnson?

alt.sports.hockey.nhl.ny-rangers

Type of Service	Newsgroup
Category	Sports
Description	New York Rangers hockey talk

Review

Sure they won the Stanley Cup, but are the fans satisfied? With Mike Keenan playing the weasel and Madison Square Garden (and all its requisite teams) being sold, the corporate powers are making one thing clear—they know little or nothing about running professional sports teams. This newsgroup is rife with controversy.

clari.local.new_york

Type of Service	Newsgroup
Category	Local Information
Description	Local news (moderated)

Review

News from New York state. There's something here for everyone—from those of us who don't know what or where the state capitol is (it's Albany) to those who want to find out what goes on in Buffalo, Syracuse, or Cheektowaga.

clari.local.nyc

Type of Service	Newsgroup
Category	Local Information
Description	Local news for New York City, (moderated)

Review

Same as `clari.local.new_york`, only it focuses on the only place in New York that really matters (in City dweller's minds, anyway).

columbianet.columbia.edu

Type of Service	Gopher Server
Category	Colleges and Universities
Description	Columbia University system-wide gopher

Internet New York

Review

ColumbiaNet provides information on campus events and schedules, classes, job opportunities, topics of community interest, and so on.
The ColumbiaNet gopher contains the research areas you would expect and helpful listings of job opportunities; its community interest section focuses on AIDS, diversity and guidelines for civil speech and conduct, and a bunch of other politically correct topics.

`cwis.nyu.edu`

Type of Service	Gopher Server
Category	Colleges and Universities
Description	NYU campus-wide information system

Review

Anything and everything about NYU is located at this gopher site. The table of contents lists almost every educational department and student/faculty service that is available.
Prospective students need only search this gopher to discover if NYU is the school that meets their needs. The educational information available clearly demonstrates how much NYU has to offer to its surrounding physical and electronic community.

`echonyc.com`

Type of Service	Gopher Server
Category	Local Information
Description	New York City information

Part II

Review

According to Stacy Horn, the ECHO gopher's creator, the ECHO server is like "an electronic cultural salon, like Gertrude Stein's living room in Paris."

ECHO list events that it sponsors. Moreover, cultural, film, music, "cool stuff," women's, queer, and Internet resources are there to be explored. And yes, there's stuff for geeks as well. Most all New Yorkers can find something of interest or of help here (wow, even the geeks!).

More than just information bytes, ECHO is a place to discuss and ponder the vagaries that are New York City. Besides finding out what's hot in New York, you can find out WHY particular sites, resources, movements, songs, books, and so on, are all the rage. Eclectic and eccentric, this is raw data with a human touch.

Some of the following entries are examples of what you can find within the ECHO gopher. The repeated addresses are not typos. To get to these sites, gopher to the ECHO server and click on the various folders that you wish to explore.

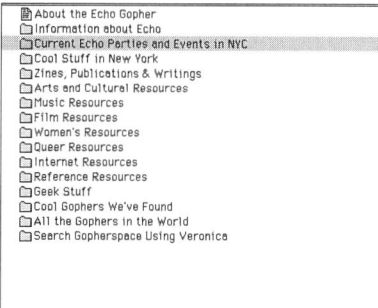

17

echonyc.com

Type of Service	Gopher Server
Category	Restaurants
Description	Restaurant reviews, listings, and more

Review

Here you'll be given directions and, more importantly, reasons for venturing into New York's neighborhoods. People want to eat out at places that remind them of home, where the glitterati gather around the trough, where the food is authentic, or where the restaurant is recognized as the "best" by a majority of one. If one New Yorker says it is the best, then it simply is, just dig in—don't fight it.

echonyc.com

Type of Service	Gopher Server
Category	Things to Do
Description	Arts and Cultural Resources

Review

A perfect guide to the SOHO art scene. This site contains a comprehensive list of museums and art galleries. Be sure to check out the Whitney Museum (all of its locations in the city).

echonyc.com

Type of Service	Gopher Server
Category	Computers
Description	Geek Stuff

Part II

Review

Items for the... socially challenged? Actually, it's good source for computer software and information. Contains listings of sites in which you can obtain software from around the world.
Helpful info for the computer jock, geek, or techno-weenie—whichever the case may be.

---

gopher.ucc.cuny.edu

Type of Service	Gopher Server
Category	Colleges and Universities
Description	CUNY, City University of New York, information gopher

Review

The CUNY gopher provides system-wide access to academic resources such as libraries (CUNYLA, the New York Public Library, and the Library of Congress), educational grant information, and the following New York State Government information: Contract information, Archives and Records, Department of Health, Department of Education, Higher Education, and access to the state's Executive, Judicial, and Legislative branches via the TNT Gopher.

The CUNY Gopher provides excellent coverage and access to educational opportunities in New York City, as well as insight into State Government. Access to its vast library system, as well as the New York Public Library system, make it a very inviting repository for those of us doing research, academic work, or merely browsing the vast resources available here.

```
http://branch.com/
```

Type of Service	World-Wide Web
Category	Reference
Description	Branch Information Services Electronic Mall

Review

It's the original 1950s Burp gun!! Exciting, safe, and totally disgusting!! You haven't had this much fun since grandma sat on that Whoopee cushion. Whee! The burp gun is one of the many different items you can find at the Branch Information Services Electronic Mall. Categories include: services, real estate, government, and miscellaneous. Be sure to check each category carefully, as online flower shops and the Burp gun are found under the same category. Good marketing or interesting categorization techniques? You make the call.

```
http://emall.com/ExploreNY/NY1.html
```

Type of Service	World-Wide Web
Category	Local Information
Description	Explore New York

Review

This is (literally) an online tour guide. All the major sights and points of interest are listed in a fairly brief, written form. Skip the annoying, over-enthusiastic, overcharged tour guide, and browse through Explore New York to help you sort out this maze of a city (Upper East Side, Upper West Side, Downtown, Midtown, Broadway, Central Park, and so forth). History and interesting facts are also provided.

Part II

```
http://nyweb.com
```

Type of Service   World-Wide Web

Category   Local Information

Description   New York City's Web browser

Review

A comprehensive guide to the city. Unlike Explore New York, the New York Web is more for the resident than the tourist (although this is very helpful for tourists as well). This site is divided into five main categories (City Life, Nite Life, Expo, Media, and Mailbox), each of which takes you to an interactive menu or it points you to another, more specific location.

The site is also very user friendly. For example, say you want to see live music at a club Friday night. Simply click the Nite Life button and then click Clubs. Wait for the interactive menu to appear, then check the boxes next to a day of the week and what you want to do (check Fridays and Live Music), and then click Submit. A listing of clubs and their Friday billing appears on your screen along with options to receive more information.

Internet New York

And remember, in New York the day of the week is very important... some places are very diverse in their clientele—offering "special" nights that cater to different groups.

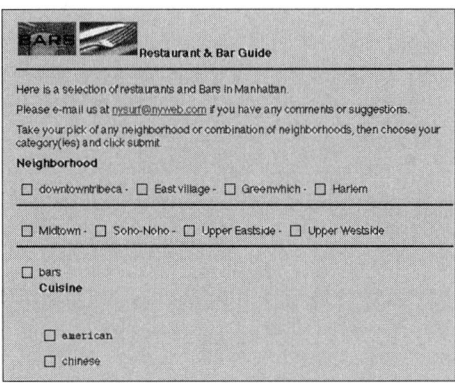

The same pick-and-choose type deal is available for many of these options, like restaurants. The Restaurants interactive menu allows you to select the neighborhood you would like to visit, along with the type of food you would like to eat. After you select these, you'll get a listing of eateries and watering holes that meet your criteria, as well as directions to the restaurant and what you can expect to find there.

Part II

The mailbox option (on the Main Menu) enables you to subscribe to the listings and have them sent to your email address. This way you'll only have to go through the web navigation process once to get what you want.

---

http://wings.buffalo.edu/world/
nywww.html

Type of Service   World-Wide Web

Category   Reference

Description   World-Wide Web servers in New York

Review

You know they are out there, but where? How do you find them? Just hit this interactive map with its pointers to Web Servers in the New York state metropolitan area. There's a lot more out there than you might think. Just let yourself get tangled. Not all of these are listed in this book, as they may not be specifically about New York.

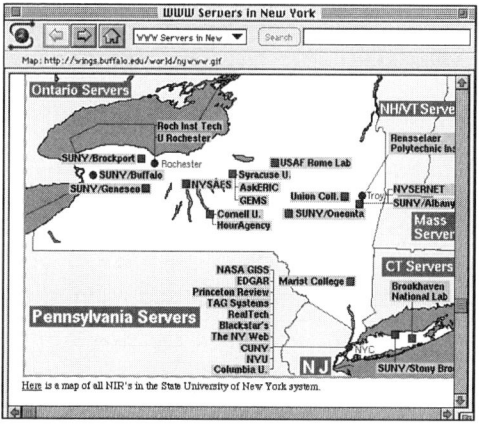

Internet New York

http://www.cs.columbia.edu/nyc/home/gr_ismap.html

Type of Service   World-Wide Web

Category   Local Information

Description   Columbia University Web—New York Information

Review

On top of everything else Columbia University has to offer, it now boasts one of the most complete listings of sites and services for tourists and natives of NYC: Current Events, Transportation, TV & Radio, Survival Guide, Sights, Museums, Food/Dining, Entertainment, Hotels & Lodging, Street Locator, and so on.

The information in these categories is very detailed. Besides complete listings, items are organized geographically, making it easy to navigate the city and make the most of any daily sojourn.

Neat stuff: An address locator to make sense out of NYC's concept of new math :-)

The server's graphical subway and bus maps will make you think twice about grabbing a cab.

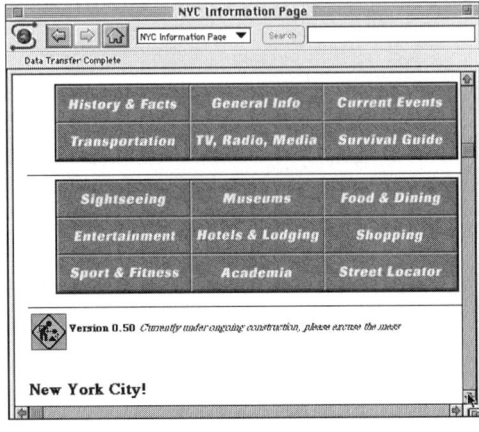

Part II

http://www.cs.columbia.edu/nyc/

Type of Service   World-Wide Web

Category   Reference

Description   NYC Information Page

Review

"Paperless Guide to New York City"
New York should be voted the city most likely to be continued on the next page. It is so diverse in its cultures, histories, and tradition that one web page can never be enough.

This web page is based on a grid structure containing the following topics: History & Facts, General Info, Current Events, Transportation, TV-Radio-Media, Survival Guide, Sightseeing, Museums, Food & Dining, Entertainment, Hotels & Lodging, Shopping, Sport & Fitness, Academia, and Street Locator.

New Yorkers are astounded by the fact that out-of-towners, especially from Chicago, cannot figure out Manhattan street addresses. You'd think it would be clearly evident that for addresses on Broadway, you cancel the last figure of the address and divide by 2. And then for addresses between 754 to 786, subtract 29. Between 847 to 953, subtract 25. And above 953, subtract 31.

It's as easy as 1, 2, 5.

Even with the street locator, you'd never figure that Waverly could meet Waverly. Ask a cab driver to take you to that intersection… Good luck! See ya in the next life.

Internet New York

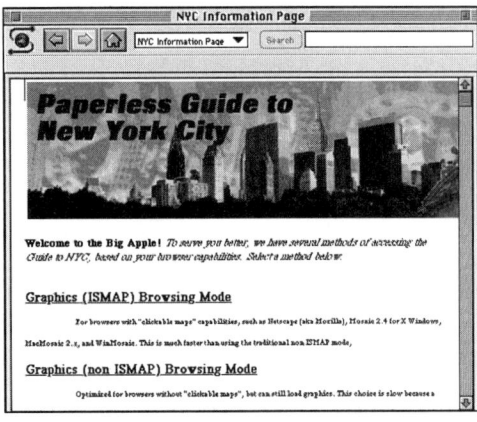

http://www.cs.columbia.edu/nyc/
transportation/subways

Type of Service   World-Wide Web

Category   Reference

Description   New York City subway system

Review

Outside of New York, you'll hear all these weird and wonderful stories about the New York City subways. Most of these stories are probably authored by cab drivers. The subway belies its name: it runs both below and above ground. It is the most efficient mass transit system in the world given the volume of people it carries. You can't beat it in the fight against cross-town traffic. Just try getting from the eastside to the westside by cab without flinching at the ticks on the meter. Just don't plan on keeping your wallet if you ride through bad neighborhoods late at night.

Part II

NYC now has metrocards. They have not been hacked yet, but give our East Coast hackers time. Using the subway picker you can scan a map of the system, pick an area you'd like to travel, and then have it blown up on screen so you can print it out or save it out to a file.

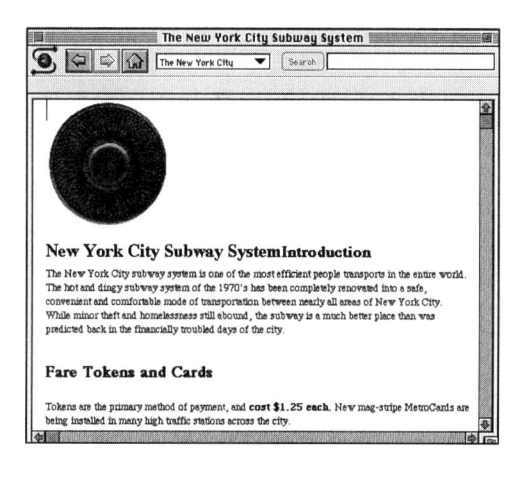

New York City Subway System Introduction

The New York City subway system is one of the most efficient people transports in the entire world. The hot and dingy subway system of the 1970's has been completely renovated into a safe, convenient and comfortable mode of transportation between nearly all areas of New York City. While minor theft and homelessness still abound, the subway is a much better place than was predicted back in the financially troubled days of the city.

Fare Tokens and Cards

Tokens are the primary method of payment, and cost **$1.25 each**. New mag-stripe MetroCards are being installed in many high traffic stations across the city.

---

http://www.cshl.org/

Type of Service	World-Wide Web
Category	Reference
Description	Cold Spring Harbor Laboratory Information Online (CLIO)

Review

Cold Spring Harbor is an non-profit, independent research and educational institution chartered by the State University of New York. It serves as a research, training, experimentation, communication, and publishing facility for, and about, scientists and science.

Internet New York

http://www.mcs.com/~bliss/
starchild/soundadvice.html

Type of Service   World-Wide Web

Category   Hobbies

Description   Sound Advice—quartet playing alternative/progressive rock

Review

Planet Starchild II is an online indie music catalog. Sound Advice is but one entry in the catalog. With the proper graphics/audio viewer, you can sample their music and video.
For more info on this Online MultiMedia Catalog of Indie Music and More... contact **tacosurf@aol.com**

http:/www.mit.edu:8001/afas/
athena/user/e/n/enolagay/www/
nerony/n-home.

Part II

Type of Service	World-Wide Web
Category	Hobbies
Description	Nero Ashbury live action roleplaying

Review

"You adjust your boots, make sure your dagger is handy, and start walking at a leisurely pace over to the Dragon's Flagon, but only get a few steps before something jumps out at you. It's a goblin! You can tell by the ugly green face and orange mohawk." Ah yes, the ugly green face and orange mohawk. I keep forgetting how to tell a goblin from the blue-mohawk monsters. Thanks for the orange mohawk tip. Write this down in your "Monster Identification Handbook."
Definitely for those who find navigating in and around New York City mundane and predictable. These are hearty folk.

http://www.nando.net/baseball/bbs/bbhome/nym.html

Type of Service	World-Wide Web
Category	Sports
Description	New York Mets Web site

Review

Everything New York Mets. Topics include: Today's game (with box scores and recap), Metros (team notes and quotes), Statistics (team stats, league leaders, National League standings, and schedules), and team history and information.
This site was still being built at press time, but should be ready for the 1995 season (of course, who

Internet New York

knows if the players and owners will be!). However, you can still go to the site and get information on the team; just don't expect all portions of the site to be ready for browsing.

http://www.nando.net/baseball/bbs/bbhome/nyy.html

Type of Service	World-Wide Web
Category	Sports
Description	New York Yankees Web site

Review

More information than an overpriced program can give you. Topics include: Today's game (with box scores and recap), Yankee Doodles (team notes and quotes), Statistics (team stats, league leaders, American League standings, schedules), and team history and information.
This site was still being built at press time, however, it should be ready for the 1995 season. You can still go to the site and get information on the team; just don't expect all portions of the site to be ready for browsing.

http://www.nando.net/sports/bkb/1994/nba/home/nyk.html

Type of Service	World-Wide Web
Category	Sports
Description	New York Knicks Web site

Review

Hey, did you know that if you put the names of New York teams together you could make a sentence that

says "Giant Nick Met Ranger Bill"?
Topics on the Knicks site include: Today's action (recent game recap, recent game summary, feature stories and between-game reports, archive of '94-'95 game stories, box scores, and statistics), Knicks notes (Knicks-related notes and quotes), Statistics (current team statistics, team roster, NBA standings, league leaders, and a 1994 Knicks schedule), and team history and information.

Portions of this server were not complete at press time. However, much of the server is ready to give you all the information you need to know about the Knicks.

---

http://www.nando.net/football/1994/nfl/fbhome/buf.html

Type of Service	World-Wide Web
Category	Sports
Description	Buffalo Bills Web site

Review

The bill on the Bills. Topics include a recap of the week's game, game statistics, feature stories and between-game reports, archive game stories and statistics, a preview and key matchups for the next game, Buffalo Bits (Bills related notes and quotes), statistics (team statistics, team roster, NFL standings, league leaders, and the Bills' schedule), and team history and information.

Portions of this server were not complete at press time. However, much of the server is ready to give you all the information you need to know about the Bills.

Internet New York

http://www.nando.net/football/1994/nfl/fbhome/nyg.html

Type of Service	World-Wide Web
Category	Sports
Description	New York Giants Web site

Review

A Giants' fan's haven. Topics include a recap of the week's game, game statistics, feature stories and between-game reports, archive game stories and statistics, a preview and key matchups for the next game, Giant Gestures (notes and quotes from the Giants), statistics (team statistics, team roster, NFL standings, league leaders, and the Giants schedule), and team history and information.

Portions of this server were not complete at press time. However, much of the server is ready to give you all the information you need to know about the New York Giants.

http://www.nando.net/football/1994/nfl/fbhome/nyj.html

Type of Service	World-Wide Web
Category	Sports
Description	New York Jets Web site

Review

Just what the armchair (whoops, I mean keyboard) quarterback ordered. Topics include a recap of the week's game, game statistics, feature stories and between game reports, archive game stories and statistics, a preview and key matchups for the next game, Jet fuel (notes and quotes from the Jets), statistics (team statistics, team roster, NFL standings,

league leaders, and the Jets schedule), and team history and information.
Portions of this server were not complete... well, you get the idea.

http://www.tagsys.com/Ads/
FreeSpirit/resaurant.html

Type of Service   World-Wide Web

Category   Restaurants

Description   Vegetarian restaurant listings

Review

This site lists three categories of vegetarian restaurants in the five boroughs of New York City: totally vegetarian, vegetarian with fish and/or dairy, and not totally vegetarian. However, this site does not include reviews of the restaurants, it includes only listings by category and addresses of the restaurants. Eat at your own risk.

ny.forsale

Type of Service   Newsgroup

Category   Local Information

Description   Items for sale in New York

Review

Most of the items you'll find here are mechanical items. Cars, computer hardware, and musical instruments seem to be the most popular items that New Yorkers want to get rid of.
This is a good place to check before you spend too much money at one of the overpriced stores in the City, or if you can't get enough information from

the ads in the newspapers. These ads don't have a space limit, so descriptions can be as long as the seller chooses.

ny.politics

Type of Service	Newsgroup
Category	Local Information
Description	New York political discussions

Review

Discussions and arguments are rampant. A sounding board for New York activists, politicians, and campaigns. This is an excellent place to find heated discussions over minor and major political issues.

ny.seminars

Type of Service	Newsgroup
Category	Local Information
Description	New York and national seminars

Review

Not a real popular list, but you never know what you can find. Topics are diverse, but discussions are nonexistent.

nyc.announce

Type of Service	Newsgroup
Category	Local Information
Description	NYC announcements

Part II

Review

The town crier may have given way to radio and television, but OYEZ! He's back. Just check out the announcements in this group for computer meetings, gallery openings, nostalgia for sale, band gigs, the kitchen sink....

nyc.food

Type of Service   Newsgroup

Category   Restaurants

Description   NYC food

Review

You can't go hungry in New York (well, unless you're broke, then you *will* go hungry in New York). And with more restaurants than you can shake a pair of chopsticks at, this is where you can find out about new restaurants, exchange recipes, locate the freshest produce and choicest meats, and much more.
By sampling the ethnic delicacies of the city, you can travel the world and still come home every night. This group is your roadmap to these great stores, foods, and restaurants.

nyc.general

Type of Service   Newsgroup

Category   Local Information

Description   All things New York City

Internet New York

Review

Like the City, this newsgroup is active 24/7 (24 hours a day, 7 hours a week). Before reading this newsgroup, keep a few things in mind: everything is fair game, New Yorkers are opinionated, and everybody is right. Grasp these concepts and you'll feel right at home.

nyc.seminars

Type of Service	Newsgroup
Category	Local Information
Description	New York City and national seminars

Review

Same as `ny.seminars`, only different.

nyplgate.nypl.org

Type of Service	Telnet
Category	Reference
Description	New York Public Library

Review

Between the great lions are an awesome number of books, documents, periodicals, and more. This long-distance connection to the largest public library in the United States (after the Library of Congress) lets your fingers do the walking among the myriad of stacks and carrels. Login as NYPL, no password is needed, not even a library card… and you can be as loud as you want. No more fussy librarians. Ahhhh.

panix.com

Type of Service	Gopher Server
Category	Reference
Description	New York information

Review

The MIT Guide to Lock Picking was found on this server at press time. That's funny. Who would have thought that you'd find a lock picking guide on a New York server? Who in New York would want to pick a lock?
Hmm.
Also available are guides to New York City places, organizations, and information, an artists guide, a photography database, and so on. A neat guide for the abstract.

spinaltap.micro.umn.edu

Type of Service	Gopher
Category	Hobbies
Description	Comprehensive New York City bookstore list

Review

Found in the /pub/games/newyorkcity at the University of Minnesota gopher, this list covers literary haunts both downtown and uptown. Complete with descriptions of the shops' contents. The creators of this list have included both new and used bookstores, so bargains abound.

Internet New York

timessqr.gc.cuny.edu

Type of Service	Gopher Server
Category	Colleges and Universities
Description	CUNY, City University of New York, Graduate Center Experimental Gopher

Review

Open the folder titled "About New York City," and you'll receive an online guide to the city. This guide contains fully documented lists of where, when, and what to do in New York City. The descriptions lists are broken down into the following categories:
Bars and Pubs/
Bookstores Guide/
Clubs/
Facts about New York City
Hotels Information/
Music/
NYC Museums/
New York Francophone
Restaurant Guide/
Sports/
Theater Guide/Press
The next eight addresses go into more detail for each of these categories.

timessqr.gc.cuny.edu

Type of Service	Gopher Server
Category	Night Life
Description	CUNY, City University of New York, Graduate Center Experimental Gopher Bars and Pubs/

Part II

Review

Contributors to the bar and pub listings are solicited and welcome. Drinking establishments are classified by their location: Downtown/Lower East Side/MidTown/SoHo/Upper East Side/Upper West Side/Greenwich Village. Given the CUNY Graduate Center's location in Manhattan, it should be of little surprise that the bar and pub listings are decidedly of the "island" borough.

timessqr.gc.cuny.edu

Type of Service	Gopher Server
Category	Hobbies
Description	CUNY, City University of New York, Graduate Center Experimental Gopher Bookstores Guide/

Review

Spanning Manhattan, Brooklyn, and Queens, the bookstore list classifies sites by their location. Each entry provides a phone number and brief description of the genre of books to be found within.

timessqr.gc.cuny.edu

Type of Service	Gopher Server
Category	Night Life
Description	CUNY, City University of New York, Graduate Center Experimental Gopher Clubs/

Review

The phrase "Clubbing in New York" may take on two meanings, but we'll concern ourselves with the more civilized notion. There are lots of clubs in New York City, some making their mark on the city for years, others stay only long enough to make weekly club listings obsolete.

As is the case with lists in this gopher, their content depends upon the kindness of strangers to offer vital statistics. Each entry will tell you where to find the club, phone number, food/drink, and whether or not the joint is jumping.

timessqr.gc.cuny.edu

Type of Service	Gopher Server
Category	Reference
Description	CUNY, City University of New York, Graduate Center Experimental Gopher Facts About New York City/

Review

More than 587 miles of waterfront, 6,400 miles of streets, 14.3 miles of beaches, 1,543 parks and playgrounds, comprising 26,138 acres... just some of the reasons tourists visit the Big Apple. There are a lot more arcane factoids here, which if nothing else, will make even the most inveterate "hick" seem positively cosmopolitan or at least metropolitan. Amuse your friends, terrify your neighbors with your mastery of NYC trivia.

timessqr.gc.cuny.edu

Type of Service	Gopher Server
Category	Reference
Description	CUNY, City University of New York, Graduate Center Experimental Gopher Hotels Information/

Review

There are 8,000,000 stories in the "Naked City" and there are almost as many hotel rooms. These run the gamut on scales of luxury, price, and convenience. This hotel guide also covers: handicap access, children's policy, health club, and package deals. Phone and fax numbers are there to make reservations as soon as you find the right hotel to fit your needs.

timessqr.gc.cuny.edu

Type of Service	Gopher Server
Category	Museums
Description	CUNY, City University of New York, Graduate Center Experimental Gopher NYC Museums/

Review

New Yorkers have so much at their disposal that they tend to take some things for granted. There are more than 150 museums in and around the city. Exhibits are from all over the world, ranging from ancient to modern. Admission prices vary. Best bet is to call the museums.
Location, phone numbers, and the museum's focus are all listed.

Internet New York

timessqr.gc.cuny.edu

Type of Service	Gopher Server
Category	Reference
Description	CUNY, City University of New York, Graduate Center Experimental Gopher New York Francophone/

Review

New York City is a mix of immigrants from everywhere, including France. This unique guide contains information on French speaking television/radio programs, stores, cinemas, plays, and more....
No doubt there will be guides for other ethnic groups in the future.

timessqr.gc.cuny.edu

Type of Service	Gopher Server
Category	Theaters
Description	CUNY, City University of New York, Graduate Center Experimental Gopher Theater Guide/Press

Review

Never ask a city dweller for their opinion on a Broadway show, because more often than not they have put off going to the show until it is too late and the run is over. Jaded as they may be, price is also a factor as ticket prices have skyrocketed, but do not despair.

Part II

New York City boast two TKTS reduced price ticket booths. Savvy shoppers can get discounts from 25 to 50 percent off Broadway and Off-Broadway shows. There is a $2.50 service charge.
Check the decidedly low-tech daily *New York Times* for play listings, and the world's your oyster at a discount.

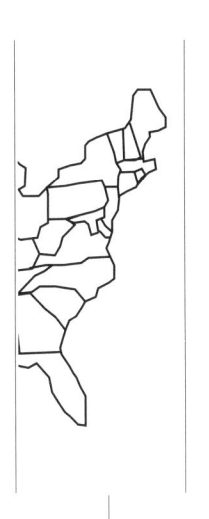

Part III

Internet Providers

In order to connect to the Internet, you need an Internet provider. Providers will, for a fee, connect you to the Internet through your modem. The types of connections vary, but you'll really want to have full access (through TCP/IP) so that you can take advantage of everything the Internet has to offer.

The number of service providers changes almost daily, and you may find that some of the following information is out-of-date. This is unfortunate, but this list will certainly give you enough information to find a good provider.

The providers listed are broken down into two major sections: New York area providers and national providers. Obviously, New York area providers are located in the New York area. National providers have access points all over the country and have 212, 718, or 800 area code dial-up numbers. Be sure to check both sections as you may find that a national provider's service is more appropriate for you.

Following is a key to the provider listing:

Address Mailing address of the service provider.

Service Areas Areas in which the service provider has local dialing service available. If you can dial one of these numbers without incurring a long distance charge, then you probably will not have telephone charges (in addition to any connect time charges or fees).

Public Access Some providers utilize public access methods to hook into their network. Typically these public access providers have local phone numbers nationally. Check with the provider to see if there is a local access point in your area.

Access Method This is the *type* of Internet connection. The best mechanisms from a UNIX host, PC, or Macintosh will be a SLIP or PPP connection (so you will be able to take advantage of Internet programs that use a graphical user interface). Shell and BBS are simply terminal-level access. UUCP is typically email. Leased Lines and Frame Relay are LAN-based connections.

Domain The domain name for the service provider. If you are given electronic mail, you may get an address of the form *username*@*domain.*

Information This item contains voice and/or fax numbers for the service provider. These are not modem lines, so don't try to connect to these numbers.

Guest Account For Telnet or terminal-level access, some providers have a *guest account,* which allows you to sample some of the services or sign up for service.

FTP Server Some Internet providers have an FTP site. There may be publicly available files under the *anonymous* account. Subscribers may also have their own ftp directories. The ftp server's IP address is also listed.

World-Wide Web Some providers have a web server that you can access. If so, this item gives the address of the home page that may provide company information, background, services available, and related information.

New York Area Providers

Dorsai

Address	Dorsai Embassy
Service Areas	Long Island City
Public Access	None

Internet New York

Access Method	Shell: elm, gopher, archie, WAIS, IRC
Domain	dorsai.org
Information	(718) 729-4208
Electronic Mail	info@dorsai.dorsai.org
Guest Account	(718) 729-5339 modem; login *new*
FTP Server	None
World-Wide Web	None

Echo

Address	Echo Communications Group, Inc.
Service Areas	New York City
Public Access	SprintNet, PSINet
Access Method	SLIP PPP BBS
Domain	echonyc.com
Information	(212) 255-3839 (212) 627-5191 (FAX)
Electronic Mail	horn@echonyc.com
Guest Account	(212) 989-3382 modem; login *newuser*
FTP Server	None
World-Wide Web	None

Maestro

Address	Maestro Technologies 29 John Street, Suite 1601 New York, NY 10038

Part III

Service Areas	New York City
Public Access	None
Access Method	Shell: gopher, archie, WAIS, IRC, mail, news
Domain	maestro.com
Information	(212) 240-9600
Electronic Mail	info@maestro.com
Guest Account	(212) 240-9700 modem; login *newuser*
FTP Server	None
World-Wide Web	None

MindVox

Address	Phantom Access Technologies, Inc. 175 Fifth Avenue, Suite 2614 New York, NY
Service Areas	New York City
Public Access	SprintNet
Access Method	Shell: gopher, archie, WAIS, IRC, mail, news, menu SLIP PPP
Domain	phantom.com
Information	(212) 989-2418 (212) 989-8648 FAX
Electronic Mail	info@phantom.com
Guest Account	(212) 989-4141 modem; login *mindvox,* password *guest*

Internet New York

FTP Server	None
World-Wide Web	http://www.phantom.com

Panix

Address	Public Access Networks Corporation 110 Riverside Drive New York, NY 10024
Service Areas	Fort Lee, Hoboken, Jersey City, Nassau, New York City
Public Access	Planned
Access Method	Shell: menu, news, gopher, archie, WAIS, IRC SLIP PPP
Domain	panix.com
Information	(212) 787-6160 (212) 877-4854 (Voice Mail)
Electronic Mail	info@panix.com
Guest Account	(212) 787-3100 modem; login *help*
FTP Server	None
World-Wide Web	http://www.panix.com

Pipeline

Address	The Pipeline Network, Inc. 150 Broadway, Suite 1710 New York, NY 10038
Service Areas	New York City
Public Access	None

Access Method	Shell: menu, news, gopher, archie, WAIS, IRC Pipeline for Windows SLIP PPP ISDN
Domain	`pipeline.com`
Information	(212) 267-3636 (718) 237-0625 FAX
Electronic Mail	`info@pipeline.com`
Guest Account	(212) 267-8606 modem; login *guest*
FTP Server	`ftp.pipeline.com` [198.80.32.3]
World-Wide Web	`http://www.pipeline.com`

National Providers

JvNCnet

Address	Global Enterprise Services Princeton Corporate Center 3 Independence Way Princeton, NJ 08540
Service Areas	Hayward CA, Bridgeport CT, Ward Place DC, Downers Grove IL, Newark NJ, Princeton NJ, New York NY, Philadelphia PA, Providence RI
Public Access	None
Access Method	Shell SLIP PPP
Domain	`jvnc.com`

Internet New York

Information	(609) 897-7300 (609) 258-2424 FAX
Electronic Mail	`info@jvnc.net`
FTP Server	`ftp.jvnc.net` [128.121.50.2]
World-Wide Web	None

Netcom

Address	Netcom On-Line Communication Service 4000 Moorpark Avenue, Suite 209 San Jose, CA 95117
Service Areas	Phoenix AZ, Alameda CA, Colma CA, Culver City CA, Fair Oaks CA, Palo Alto CA, Pasadena CA, Pleasonton CA, San Diego CA, San Ramon CA, Santa Ana CA, Santa Clara CA, Santa Cruz CA, Denver CO, Atlanta GA, Park Ridge IL, Wellesley MA, Kinston NC, New York NY, Beaverton OR, Austin TX, Irving TX, Vienna VA, Seattle WA
Services	Shell: IRC, WAIS, Gopher SLIP PPP NetCruiser Frame Relay
Domain	`netcom.com`
Information	(800) 501-8649 (408) 554-8649 (408) 241-9145 FAX
Electronic Mail	`info@netcom.com`

Part III

Guest Account	(408) 261-4700 modem; login *guest* (415) 328-9940 modem; login *guest* telnet netcom.com; login *guest*
FTP Server	ftp.netcom.com [192.100.81.1]
World-Wide Web	http://www.netcom.com

PSI

Address	Performance Systems International (PSI) 11800 Sunrise Valley Drive Suite 1100 Reston, VA 22091
Service Areas	Phoenix AZ, Los Angeles CA, San Francisco CA, Santa Clara CA, Sunnyvale CA, Denver CO, Hartford CT, Stamford CT, Washington DC, Atlanta GA, Boise ID, Chicago IL, Jacksonville FL, Miami FL, Orlando FL, Tampa FL, Boston MA, Westford MA, Ann Arbor MI, Detroit MI, Mercerville NJ, Newark NJ, Princeton NJ, Buffalo, NY, Elmira NY, Garden City NY, Greenbush NY, Ithaca NY, Johnson City NY, New York NY, Potsdam NY, Poughkeepsie NY, Rochester NY, Ronkonkoma NY, Syracuse NY, Utica NY, White Plains NY, Columbus OH, Eugene OR, Portland OR, Salem OR, Philadelphia PA, Pittsburgh PA, Austin TX, Dallas TX, Houston TX, Reston VA, Seattle WA, Spokane WA

Internet New York

Services	Telnet, rlogin, Electronic Mail, feeds, FTP
Domain	`psi.com`
Information	(703) 620-6651 (703) 620-4586 FAX
Electronic Mail	`all-info@psi.com`, `pslilink-info@psi.com`
FTP Server	`ftp.psi.com` [38.145.211.6]
World-Wide Web	`http://www.psi.com`

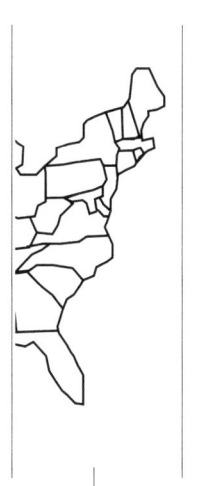

Part IV

Internet Overview

As you have seen from parts I, II, and III, the Internet offers many resources that you can use to explore your little corner of the globe as well as the whole globe itself. But, if you are a new Internet user (or old one for that matter), you may have a few questions. In this part, I will attempt to give you a brief, and thus rudimentary, understanding of this thing we call the Internet.

What I won't be able to do is to describe to you the specific software you are using or provide step-by-step instructions. That's because these vary depending upon what kind of computer you are using (PC, Mac, or UNIX) and I have no idea which kind you have. What I hope to do is to give you a general understanding of the Internet including what it is, what you can do on it, and where it came from. First up, what it is.

What is the Internet?

What is the Internet? That question is tremendously difficult to answer because the Internet is so many things to so many different people. Nonetheless, you need a short answer to give your mother when she asks, so here goes:

The Internet consists of a mind-bogglingly huge number of participants, connected machines, software programs, and a massive quantity of information, spread all around the world.

Now, let's see if I can put those various parts into some kind of meaningful context.

The Seattle Kingdome seats approximately 60,000 people for a sell-out Seahawks football or Mariners baseball game (once-in-a-lifetime experiences for those teams). That's about the same number of people who read a single, mildly popular newsgroup on the Internet. If all 23 million people on the Internet were to get together, they'd need almost 400 stadiums each the size of the Kingdome to have a party. I could calculate how many times that

Part IV

number of people would reach to the moon and back if we stacked them one on top of another, but I think I've made my point.

Explaining the geographic size of the Internet is difficult, because in many ways, messages traveling over the network connections don't give a hoot where they are going. Almost every industrialized nation (that's some 60 countries) has at least one machine on the Internet, and more countries come online all the time.

I personally prefer to think of the Internet as millions of people constantly communicating about every topic under the sun. The amount and type of information, the hardware, and the software will all change, but the simple fact of people communicating will always exist on the Internet. For example, during the Gulf War, while people in the U.S. were glued to their television sets watching the devastation, people in Israel were sending reports to the net. Some of these described the terror of air raid sirens and worrying about SCUD missiles launched from Iraq. No television shot of a family getting into their gas masks with an obligatory sound bite can compare with the lengthy and tortured accounts of daily life that came from the Israeli net community.

And of course, there needs to be some media to make sure these communications get through. These media are called host machines. You can think of an Internet host machine as a large post office in a large metropolitan area. In that post office, huge quantities of information are dispensed every day, but it doesn't just gush out the front door. No, you have to go inside, sometimes wait in line, and then go to the appropriate window to talk to the proper clerk to get the information you want. You don't necessarily pick up mail that's been held for you at the same window as you purchase a money order. Internet information works in much the same way. But on an Internet host, instead of windows, information flows through virtual ports (they're more like two-way television channels than physical SCSI ports or serial ports). A port number is, as I said, like a window in the post office—you must go to the right window to buy a money order, and similarly, you must connect to the right port number to run an Internet application. Luckily, almost all of this happens behind the scenes, so you seldom have to think about it.

So, in our hypothetical Internet post office, there are seven main windows that people use on a regular basis. There are, of course, hundreds of other windows, usually used by administrative programs or other things that people don't touch much, but we won't worry about them. The main parts to worry about are email, Usenet news, Telnet, FTP, WAIS, Gopher, and the World-Wide Web. Each provides access to different sorts of information, and most people use one or more to obtain the information they need.

Now that I've said how they're all similar, in the sense of all working through connections to the proper ports, there are some distinctions we must make between the various Internet services.

Email and Usenet news (along with MUDs and Internet Relay Chat) are forms of interpersonal communication—there is always a sender and a recipient. Depending on the type of email message or news posting, you can use different analogies to the paper world.

All of the information made available through other main parts of the Internet such as Telnet, FTP,

WAIS, Gopher, and the World-Wide Web, is more like information in libraries than interpersonal communication, in the sense that you must visit the library specifically, and once there, browse or search through the resources to find a specific piece of information. These services have much more in common with traditional publishing than email and news.

> **note** I should note that, in my eyes, the difference between browsing and searching is merely that when you're browsing, you're not looking for a specific piece of information. Perhaps you only want some background, or simply want to see what's out there. When you're searching, you usually have a particular question that you want answered.

So there you have it. A thumbnail view of the Internet. Just think of the Internet as a means for millions of people to communicate, be informed, do research, explore the world, and download software, and you'll have a pretty good mental image. But, what exactly can you do on the Internet? That, my friend, is an excellent question.

What Can You Do on the Internet?

I must tread a fine line when talking about what you can do on the Internet because the level of connection (and thus the level of service) varies widely. People who can send Internet email, for instance, may not be able to use Gopher or the World-Wide Web. The services I talk about in this section require a full TCP/IP connection to the Internet. If you don't have a full TCP/IP connection, get one. You won't regret it. (Remember that a list of Internet providers is given in part III.)

Electronic Mail

Email is used by the largest number of people on the Internet, although in terms of traffic, the heaviest volumes lie elsewhere. Almost everyone who considers himself connected to the Internet in some way can send and receive email.

Most personal exchanges happen in email because email is an inherently interpersonal form of communication. All of your email comes into your electronic mailbox, and unless you let them, no one else can easily read your mail. When you get a message from a friend via email, it's not particularly different from getting that same message, printed out and stuffed in an envelope, via snail mail. Sure, it's faster and may have been easier to send, but in essence personal email is just like personal snail mail (AKA regular paper mail).

Because it's trivial to send the same piece of email to multiple people at once, you can also use email much as you would use snail mail in conjunction with a photocopy machine. If you write a little personal newsletter about what's happening in your life and send it to all the relatives at Christmas, that's the same concept as writing a single email message and addressing it to multiple people. It's still personal mail, but just a bit closer to a form letter.

Another use of email is *mailing lists*. Sending a submission to a mailing list is much like writing for a user group or alumni newsletter. You may not know all of the people who will read your message, but it is a finite (and usually relatively small) group of people who share your interests. Mailing list messages aren't usually aimed at a specific person on the list, but are intended to discuss a topic of interest to most of the people who have joined that list. However, I don't want to imply that posting to a mailing list is like writing an article for publication, since the content of most mailing lists more resembles the editorial page of a newsletter than anything else. You'll see opinions, rebuttals, diatribes, questions, comments, and even a few answers. Everyone on the list sees every posting that comes through, and the discussions often become quite spirited.

An additional type of email most resembles those "bingo cards" that you find in the back of many magazines. Punch out the proper holes or fill in the appropriate numbered circle, return the card to the magazine, and several weeks later you'll receive the advertising information you requested. For instance, I've set up my Macintosh to send an informational file about my newsletter (called *TidBITS*) automatically to anyone in the world who sends email to a certain address (`info@tidbits.com`, in case you want to try it). A number of similar systems exist on the Internet, dispensing information on a variety of subjects to anyone who can send them email. A variant of these auto-reply systems is the *mailserver* or *fileserver*, which generally looks at the Subject line in the letter or at the body of the letter and returns the requested file. Mailservers enable people with email-only access to retrieve files that otherwise are available only via FTP.

Usenet News

Like email-based discussion lists (mailing lists), Usenet news is interpersonal information—it comes from individuals and is aimed at thousands of people around the world. Unlike email, even unlike mailing lists, you cannot find out who makes up your audience. Because of this unknown audience, posting a message to Usenet is like writing a letter to the editor of a magazine or major metropolitan newspaper with hundreds of thousands of readers. We have ways of estimating how many people read each of the thousands of Usenet groups, but the estimates are nothing more than statistical constructs (though hopefully accurate ones).

Almost everything on Usenet is a discussion of some sort, although a few groups are devoted to regular information postings, with no discussion allowed. The primary difference between Usenet news and mailing lists is that news is more efficient because each machine receives only one copy of every message. If two users on the same machine (generally multi-user mainframes or workstations at this point) read the same discussion list via email, getting the same information in news is twice as efficient. If you have a large mainframe with 100 people all reading the same group, news suddenly becomes 100 times as efficient because the machine stores only the single copy of each message, rather than each individual receiving her own copy.

In many ways, Usenet is the kitchen table of the Internet—the common ground where no subject is taboo and you must discuss everything before implementing it. In great part because of the speed at which Usenet moves (messages appear quickly and constantly, and most machines don't keep old messages for more than a week due to lack of disk space), finding information there can be difficult. Think of Usenet as a river: you must dip in to see what's available at a specific point in time because that information may disappear downstream within a few days.

Telnet

Telnet is a tough thing to describe. The best analogy I can think of is that Telnet is like an Internet modem. As with a standard modem, Telnet enables your computer to communicate with another computer somewhere else. Where you give your modem a phone number to dial, you give Telnet an Internet address to connect to. And just like a modem, you don't really do anything within Telnet itself other than make the connection—in the vernacular, you *telnet* to that remote computer. Once that connection is made, you're using the remote computer over the Internet just as though it were sitting next to you.

File Transfer Protocol (FTP)

FTP feels like it's related to Telnet, but in fact that's an illusion—the two are basic protocols on the Internet, but are not otherwise related. Where Telnet simply enables you to connect to another remote computer and run a program there, FTP enables you to connect to a remote computer and transfer files back and forth. It's really that simple.

More data is transferred via plain old FTP than by any other method on the Internet, and that's not surprising because it's a least-common denominator that almost every machine on the Internet supports. Like Telnet, you must be directly connected to the Internet while using FTP, although there are a few special FTP-by-mail services that enable you to retrieve files stored on FTP sites by sending specially formatted email messages to an FTP-by-mail server.

There are probably millions of files available via FTP on the Internet, although you may discover that many of them are duplicates because people tend to want to give users more than one way to retrieve a file. If a major file site goes down for a few days, it's nice to have a *mirror site* that has exactly the same files and can take up the slack.

FTP is extremely useful, but it can be tough to find files if you aren't sure where to look. Enter Archie.

Archie

Archie is a remarkable example of what happens when you apply simple technology to a difficult problem in an elegant way. Here is the problem: How do you find any given file on the nets if you don't already know where it's located? After all, in comparison with finding a single file on several million machines, the proverbial haystack looks tiny, and its cousin, the proverbial needle, sticks out like the sore thumb you get when you find it. In a nutshell, Archie uses normal FTP commands to get directory listings of all the files on hundreds of anonymous FTP sites around the world. It then puts these file listings into a database and provides a simple interface for searching it. That's really all there is to Archie. It's amazing that no one thought of it before.

Part IV

> **note**
> Archie was developed in early 1991 by Alan Emtage, Peter Deutsch, and Bill Heelan from the McGill University Computing Center, Canada. Development now takes place at a company founded by Deutsch and Emtage, Bunyip Information Systems. Although the basic Archie clients software is distributed freely, Bunyip sells and supports the Archie server software.

To use Archie to find a file, you simply connect to an Archie server with your Archie client software. Once connected, you ask for the file in the best way you can (sometimes you may only have a partial file name). A list of Archie servers is shown in table IV.1. As always, it's polite to choose a local server rather than a more distant one if you can.

> **note**
> Archie isn't an acronym for anything, although it took me half an hour searching through files about Archie on the Internet to determine that once and for all.

Table IV.1
Current Archie Servers

Server Name	Server IP Number	Location
archie.au	139.130.4.6	Australia
archie.edvz.uni-linz.ac.at	140.78.3.8	Austria
archie.univie.ac.at	131.130.1.23	Austria
archie.uqam.ca	132.208.250.10	Canada
archie.funet.fi	128.214.6.100	Finland

continues

Table IV.1 Continued

Server Name	Server IP Number	Location
archie.th-darmstadt.de	130.83.22.60	Germany
archie.ac.il	132.65.6.15	Israel
archie.unipi.it	131.114.21.10	Italy
archie.wide.ad.jp	133.4.3.6	Japan
archie.kr	128.134.1.1	Korea
archie.sogang.ac.kr	163.239.1.11	Korea
archie.rediris.es	130.206.1.2	Spain
archie.luth.se	130.240.18.4	Sweden
archie.switch.ch	130.59.1.40	Switzerland
archie.ncu.edu.tw	140.115.19.24	Taiwan
archie.doc.ic.ac.uk	146.169.11.3	United Kingdom
archie.unl.edu	129.93.1.14	USA (NE)
archie.internic.net	198.48.45.10	USA (NJ)
archie.rutgers.edu	128.6.18.15	USA (NJ)
archie.ans.net	147.225.1.10	USA (NY)
archie.sura.net	128.167.254.179	USA (MD)

WAIS

WAIS (Wide Area Information Search) originated from a company called Thinking Machines but has now split off into its own company, WAIS, Inc. Using the tremendous processing power of Thinking Machines' Connection Machine supercomputer or another powerful computer, WAIS can quickly (usually under a minute) return a number of articles to English-language queries, sorted by the likelihood that they are relevant to your question. WAIS is limited only by the information that people feed into it.

Last I counted, there were over 500 sources available for searching within topics as diverse as Buddhism, cookbooks, song lyrics, Supreme Court decisions, science fiction book reviews, and President Clinton's speeches. For all the sources on non-technical topics, I'm sure an equal number exist about technical topics in many fields.

Perhaps the hardest part about WAIS is learning how to ask it questions. Even though you can use natural English queries, it takes your question quite literally, and only applies it to the selected sources. So, if you asked about deforestation in the Amazon rainforest while searching in the Buddhism source, I'd be surprised if you found anything. Perhaps the most generically useful server is the Connection-Machine server, which includes the 1990 CIA World Factbook, a few patents, some biology abstracts, the King James Version of the Bible, the NIH Guide to Grants and Programs, the PARIS manual for programming the Connection Machine, a number of public mailing lists including *TidBITS* and the Info-Mac Digest, and a couple of months of the *Wall Street Journal* (but the issues are old).

Gopher

Gopher, which originated with the Golden Gophers of the University of Minnesota, is an information browser along the same lines as FTP, but with significant enhancements for ease of use and flexibility. Numerous sites—more than 1,500 at last count—on the Internet run the host Gopher software, placing information in what are colloquially called *gopher holes*. When you connect to a Gopher site, you can search databases, read text files, transfer files, and generally navigate around the collection of gopher holes, which is itself called *Gopherspace*.

I find Gopher to be the most useful of the Internet services in terms of actually making information available that I need to answer specific questions. Part of the reason for my opinion is *Veronica*, and to a lesser extent *Jughead*, which enable you to search through Gopherspace as Archie enables you to search for files on anonymous FTP servers.

> **note** *Veronica* and *Jughead* were both named to match *Archie* (from the Archie comics), but Veronica's creators at the University of Nevada did come up with an acronym as well—Very Easy Rodent-Oriented Net-wide Index to Computerized Archives. Jughead stands for Jonzy's Universal Gopher Hierarchy Excavation And Display. Glad you asked?

Veronica searches through all of Gopherspace, which is useful, although badly phrased searches (Veronica doesn't use natural English, as WAIS does) can result in hundreds of results. Jughead searches a subset of Gopherspace and can thus be more accurate, though less comprehensive.

One of the special features of Gopher is that it provides access to FTP (and Archie) and WAIS, and can even run a Telnet program to provide access to resources only available via Telnet. Gopher can also work with other programs to provide access to special data types, such as pictures and sounds. When you double-click on a picture listing in Gopher, it downloads the file and then runs another program to display the picture. This sort of integration doesn't generally work all that well if what you have is UNIX command-line access to the Internet.

Part IV

World-Wide Web

Since its inception a short time ago, everything about the Web has changed rapidly. It's become much, much larger, and the resources available on it have become incredibly diverse and far more useful.

> **note** You may see the World-Wide Web referred to as simply "the Web," "W3," or sometimes as "WWW."

The Web brings a couple of very important features to the Internet. First, unlike Gopher or anything else, it provides access to full fonts, sizes, and styles for text, and can include images onscreen with no special treatment. Sounds and movies are also possible, though often too large for many people to download and view. Second, the Web provides true hypertextual links between documents anywhere on the Web, not just on a single machine. For those unfamiliar with hypertext, it's a powerful concept that enables the reader to navigate flexibly through linked pieces of information. If you read a paragraph with a link promising more information about the topic, say, results from last winter's Olympic Games, simply click on the link, and you'll see the results. It really is that simple, and the World-Wide Web is indeed the wave of the future for the Internet. Nothing touches it in terms of pure attractiveness, although many Web servers that you see suffer from the same problem that many publications did after the Macintosh made desktop-publishing popular: they're designed by amateurs and are ugly as sin.

There is More

There are a few more things you can do on the Internet such as chatting and Multi-User Dungeons (MUDs), but I've covered the major stuff you are likely to use. (To learn the specifics of using these services, check out *Internet Starter Kit for Macintosh, Internet Explorer Kit for Macintosh, 2nd Edition,* and *Internet Starter Kit for Windows* [all Hayden Books, 1994].) Now that you know something about what the Internet is and what you can do, here's how the Internet came into being.

How Did the Internet Get Here?

Unlike the Greek goddess Athena, the Internet did not spring from the head of some Zeusian computer scientist. It was formed by a process of relatively rapid accretion and fusion (but keep in mind that this industry is one in which computer power doubles every few years). In 1980, there were 200 machines on the Internet—that number is now more than 2.3 million. The grain of sand that formed the heart of this giant electronic pearl came from the U.S. Department of Defense (DoD) in 1969. I'm pleased to be older than the Internet, having been born in 1967, but I'm not enough older to talk authoritatively about world conditions at that time. So, please bear with my second-hand retelling.

Cold War Network

In the 1950s, the Russian Sputnik program humiliated the United States. To better compete in the space race, the U.S. space program (at the time under the auspices of the military) received major government funding. That funding came from the DoD under its Advanced Research Projects Agency (ARPA). In the early 1960s, the space program left the military to become NASA, but ARPA remained, and as with many government programs that have seemingly lost their reason to exist, as did its funding. What to do with the money?

The DoD was, at that time, the world's largest user of computers, so J.C.R. Licklider and others proposed that ARPA support large-scale basic research in computer science. ARPA didn't originally require that the research it supported be either classified or directly related to military applications, which left the door open for far-reaching research in many fields. In 1963, ARPA devoted a measly $5 to $8 million to its computer research, the Information Processing Technologies Office (IPTO), first under Licklider, and then subsequently under the 26-year-old Ivan Sutherland, who had developed an early (perhaps the earliest) graphics program at MIT. After Sutherland, a 32-year-old named Robert Taylor headed IPTO. Taylor managed to double IPTO's budget in a time when ARPA's overall budget was decreasing, and even admitted to diverting funds from military-specific projects to pure computer science.

Around this time, the ARPAnet (Advanced Research Projects Agency Network) got its start, connecting various computers around the country at sites performing research for ARPA. Computers were expensive, and sharing them was the only way to distribute the resources appropriately. Distribution of cost via networks proved to be an important force in the development of the Internet later on as well. Proponents like Taylor ensured the early survival of the fledgling ARPAnet when it was all too vulnerable to governmental whimsy.

In 1969, Congress got wind of what ARPA was up to in terms of funding basic research with money from the defense budget. Three senators, including the still-active Edward Kennedy, pushed through legislation requiring that ARPA show that its programs were directly applicable to the military. In the process, ARPA's name changed to reflect its new nature; it became the Defense Advanced Research Projects Agency, or DARPA. (Years later, the name changed back to ARPA again, just to confuse the issue.) Bob Taylor became entangled in some unpleasant business reworking military computers in Saigon during the Vietnam War and left DARPA shortly thereafter. He was succeeded by Larry Roberts, who worked in large part in getting the then two-year-old ARPAnet up and running. Stewart Brand, founder of *The Whole Earth Catalog*, wrote at the time:

> At present some 20 major computer centers are linked on the two-year-old ARPA Net. Traffic on the Net has been very slow, due to delays and difficulties of translation between different computers and divergent projects. Use has recently begun to increase as researchers travel from center to center and want to keep in touch with home base, and as more tantalizing sharable resources come available. How Net usage will evolve is uncertain. There's a curious mix of theoretical fascination and operational resistance around the scheme. The resistance may have something to do with reluctance about equipping a future Big Brother and his Central Computer. The fascination resides in the thorough

rightness of computers as communication instruments, which implies some revolutions. (Stewart Brand, in *II Cybernetic Frontiers,* Random House, 1974)

So if DARPA had to justify the military applications of its research, what survived? Well, the ARPAnet did, and here's why: As leaders of the free world (pardon the rhetoric), we needed the latest and greatest methods of killing as many other people as possible. Along with *offensive* research must perforce come *defensive* research; even the DoD isn't so foolish as to assume we could wage a major war entirely on foreign soil. For this reason, the tremendous U.S. interstate highway system served double duty as distribution medium for tanks and other military hardware. Similarly, the Internet's precursor was both a utilitarian and experimental network. ARPAnet connected both military research sites (hardware was expensive and had to be shared) and was an experiment in resilient networks that could withstand a catastrophe—including, in the imaginations of the DoD planners of the day, an atomic bomb.

Interestingly, the resiliency of the ARPAnet design, as carried down to the Internet, has led some to note that the Internet routes around censorship as it would route around physical damage. It's a fascinating thought, especially in regard to Stewart Brand's earlier comment about Big Brother. If anything, the Internet actually has served to reduce the threat of a Big Brother, because it makes communication between people so fluid and unrestricted. But, I anticipate myself.

Gateways

As a result of the machinations described previously, the Internet Protocol, or IP (the second half of TCP/IP) was created. Essentially, the point behind IP systems is that each computer knows of or can determine the existence of all the others and thus route packets of information to its destination via the quickest route. While doing this, they are able to take into account any section of the network that's been bombed out or has merely been cut by an over-enthusiastic telephone repairperson. This design turns out to work well; more importantly, it makes for an extremely flexible network. If your computer can get a properly addressed packet of information to a machine on the Internet, that machine will worry about how to deliver it, translating as necessary. That's the essence of a *gateway*—it connects two dissimilar networks, translating information so that it can pass transparently from one to the other.

In the early 1980s, the military began to rely more and more heavily on the ARPAnet for communication, but because the ARPAnet still connected a haphazard mix of research institutions, businesses doing defense work, and military sites, the military wanted their own network. And so the ARPAnet split in half, becoming the ARPAnet and the Milnet (Military Network). The ARPAnet continued to carry traffic for research sites, and even though the military now had their own Milnet, traffic passed between the ARPAnet and the Milnet by going through gateways.

The concept of gateways proved important in the history of the Internet. Alongside the development of the Internet came the development of a number of other, generally smaller networks that used protocols other than IP, such as BITNET, JANET, and various others. These also included some like Usenet and CSNET that didn't care what protocols were used. These networks were regional or dedicated to serving certain types of machines or users.

Perhaps the largest driving force behind the Internet is that of the need to connect with other people and other networks. The grass is always greener on the other side of the fence, and gradually gateway sites sprung up so that email could pass between the different networks with ease.

Usenet

I'm going to take a brief break from the Internet itself, because at approximately the same time the ARPAnet split, a whole host of other networks came into being, probably the most interesting of which was Usenet, the User's Network.

Usenet started in 1979, when two graduate students at Duke decided to link several UNIX computers together in an attempt to better communicate with the rest of the UNIX community. The system they created included software to read news, post news, and transport news between machines. To this day, that simple model continues, but whereas at one time two machines were on Usenet, today there are hundreds of thousands. The software that transports and displays Usenet news now runs on not just UNIX machines, but on almost every type of computer in use on the networks. The topics of discussion have blossomed from UNIX into almost any conceivable subject—and many inconceivable ones. Like all the other network entities, Usenet quickly grew to be international in scope and size.

Unlike many of the other networks, Usenet truly grew from the bottom up, rather than from the top down. Usenet was created by and for users, and no organization—commercial, federal, or otherwise—had a hand in it originally. In many ways, Usenet has provided much of the attitude of sharing that exists on the Internet today. In the past, you usually got a Usenet *feed* (that is, had another machine send news traffic to your machine) for free (other than your telephone charges) as long as you were willing to pass the feed on to someone else for free. Due to commercial pressures, the days of the free feeds are essentially no more, but the spirit of cooperation they engendered remains in much of what happens on the Internet.

I don't want to imply that Usenet is this happy carefree network where everything is free and easy, because in many cases it's a noisy, unpleasant network that exists because of the utility of some of the information that it carries. Despite the attitude toward sharing, the survival of Usenet is due in large part to the resourcefulness of network administrators at major sites. Faced with mounting telephone charges for long distance calls between Usenet hosts, these administrators found a way to carry Usenet news over the TCP/IP-based Internet rather than just the previous modem-based UUCP connections. Thus, they prevented the costs of carrying Usenet from coming to the attention of the bean counters poised to strike unnecessary expenses from their budgets. The TCP/IP connections of the ARPAnet, and then the Internet, were already paid for. So, by figuring out how to carry Usenet over those lines, the network administrators managed to cut their costs, keep users happy, and save Usenet from itself in the process. In other words, Usenet may be an anarchy, but it wouldn't stand a chance without some occasional help from high places.

Part IV

BITNET

Shortly after Usenet took its first faltering networked steps, Ira Fuchs of City University of New York and Gleydon Freeman of Yale University decided to network their universities using IBM's then-new NJE communications protocol. Although this protocol later expanded to support Digital Equipment's Vaxen running VMS and even some implementations of UNIX, the vast majority of machines on BITNET (the "Because It's Time" network) have always been IBM mainframes. Fuchs and Freeman made their connection in the spring of 1981. BITNET grew rapidly, encompassing over 100 organizations on 225 machines by 1984, and reaching the current level of 1,400 organizations in 49 countries around the world. Most BITNET sites are at universities, colleges, and other research institutions.

BITNET has always been a cooperative network; members pass traffic bound for other sites free of charge, and software developed by one has been made available to all. Unlike Usenet, however, BITNET developed an organizational structure in 1984. This took the form of an Executive Committee, made up of representatives of all the major nodes on the network. Also in 1984, IBM provided a large grant that provided initial funding for centralized network support services. This grant, coupled with the fact that most of the machines on BITNET were IBM mainframes, gave rise to the erroneous rumor that BITNET was an IBM network. In 1987, BITNET became a nonprofit corporation. In 1989, it changed its corporate name to CREN, the Corporation for Research and Educational Networking, when it merged its administrative organization with another of the parallel educational networks, CSNET (the Computer+Science Network). Today, BITNET is in something of a decline, due in large part to the nonstandard NJE protocol in an increasingly IP world.

NSFNET

The next big event in the history of the Internet was the creation of the high-speed NSFNET (National Science Foundation Network) in 1986. NSFNET was developed to connect supercomputer sites around the country. Because supercomputers are terribly expensive, the NSF could afford to fund only five (and even then they received some major financial help from companies like IBM). With this limited number, it made sense to network the supercomputers so that researchers everywhere could use them without traveling great distances. At first, the NSF tried to use the ARPAnet, but that attempt quickly became bogged down in bureaucracy and red tape.

The NSF, therefore, decided to build its own network. Merely connecting the five supercomputer sites wasn't going to help the vast majority of researchers, of course, so the NSF created (or used existing) regional networks that connected schools and research sites in the same area. Then those networks were connected to the NSFNET.

To quote from W.P. Kinsella's *Shoeless Joe*, "If you build it, they will come." Perhaps not surprisingly, once all of these networks were able to communicate with one another, the supercomputer usage faded into the background. Other uses, most notably email, became preeminent. One of the important features of the NSFNET was that the NSF encouraged universities to provide wide access to students and staff, so the population of and traffic on the net increased dramatically.

In 1987, the NSF awarded a contract to a group of companies to manage and upgrade the NSFNET. This group was made up of IBM, MCI, and Merit Network, which ran the educational network in Michigan. The group dealt with the massive increase in traffic by replacing the old lines with much faster connections.

Eventually the NSFNET had entirely supplanted the ARPAnet, and in March of 1990, the ARPAnet was taken down for good, having played the starring role for 21 years. Similarly, another national network, CSNET, which had connected computer science researchers around the country, closed its electronic doors a year later, all of its traffic having moved to the faster NSFNET.

NREN

The NSFNET is all fine and nice, but in many ways it discriminated against "lower" education—two-year colleges, community colleges, and the much-maligned K–12 schools. To save the day, then-Senator Al Gore sponsored a bill, passed in December of 1991, called the "High-Performance Computing Act of 1991." Gore's legislation created a new network on top of (and initially using) the NSFNET. This new network is called the interim NREN, for National Research and Education Network. Along with providing even faster speeds when feasible (at which point the "interim" will go away), the NREN specifically targets grade schools, high schools, public libraries, and two- and four-year colleges. In working with the thousands of people who subscribe to *TidBITS*, I see a lot of email addresses, and it's clear to me that these educational institutions are joining the Internet in droves. A day rarely passes when I don't see something from someone whose address clearly labels him or her as a teacher at a grade school or even a student in a high school.

Alert readers probably have noticed that NREN looks a lot like CREN, and in fact, the acronyms are similar—with reason. CREN recognizes the need for an integrated National Research and Education Network. In fact, as the IBM-created NJE protocol gradually disappears in favor of the more powerful and popular IP, CREN has said it will disband, merge with NREN, or cooperate with it as appropriate—though only when NREN exists with access rules, funding, and usage policies that allow a clean transition. Currently, CREN feels that the interim NREN, the NSFNET, does not provide consistent policies regarding these issues. And, of course, what happens if commercial organizations end up running some large part of the NREN?

Who Pays?

Along with the NREN taking over the part of the Internet that was the NSFNET, more and more of the Internet is being created and run by commercial organizations. All a commercial provider has to do is pay for its part of the network, just as universities pay for their connections and government departments pay for theirs. The difference is that unlike universities or government organizations, commercial providers want to make money, or at least break even, so they in turn sell access to their machines or networks to other providers or to end users.

Part IV

The gut reaction to the commercialization of the Internet from the old-timers (who remember when you could get a Usenet feed merely by asking) is often negative, but most people believe that the Internet must accept commercial traffic. In part, this response is true because the only alternative to accepting commercial traffic is actively rejecting it, and no one wants to sit around censoring the Internet, were that even possible.

Commercialization also allows small organizations to create the equivalent of wide-area networks that previously only large businesses could afford. A company such as Microsoft can spend the money to install an international company network, but few companies are so large or so wealthy. Many may not need such an international network, but may need enhanced communications. Email can be a powerful medium for business communication, just as it is for personal communication. And, if transferring a file via FTP or email can save a few uses of an overnight courier, the connection can pay for itself in no time.

In addition, whereas in the past you had to work at a large business or university to gain Internet access, it has become far easier for an individual to get access without any such affiliation, although the costs are of course more obvious. Easier independent access couldn't have happened without increased participation by commercial interests.

The commercialization issue has another side. The U.S. government still runs the interim NREN, which is a large portion of the Internet and connects many of the major educational sites. As more commercial providers get into the business and see the massive interest in the Internet, they increasingly think that the government should turn the public portions of the Internet over to them. This thought has much support because the commercial providers could make money, which is what they want to do, and the government could save money, which is what many people want the government to do.

In fact, as I wrote the first edition of the *Internet Starter Kit*, an impassioned plea was zapping around the Internet. This plea, poorly worded and ambiguous, claimed that the government was indeed proposing to sell off the Internet—lock, stock, and barrel—which, the message claimed, could result in millions of people losing free Internet access. Coincidentally, as I wrote the second edition, another such message appeared, although this time from the Taxpayer Assets Project (TAP), a non-profit government watch organization. The TAP letter claimed that the National Science Foundation was proposing to contract with four telephone companies to provide the high-speed Internet backbone, and—the claim continued—that usage-based pricing would appear on the Internet as a result, harming the Internet in the process. In an informal rebuttal posted to a Cornell mailing list, M. Stuart Lynn, currently the head of Cornell Information Technologies, noted that the Internet is a global network and some countries, such as New Zealand, already have usage-based pricing. So even if the NSFNET moved to usage-based pricing, most of the Internet wouldn't be affected. Stuart Lynn also commented that the federal subsidy is trivial to many institutions, and at Cornell is equivalent to two cans of beer per student per year. In other words, even if Cornell had to rely on a completely commercial network (which might or might not be usage-based), its costs would not change noticeably.

Part IV

The trick is to remember that someone always pays for the Internet. If you have a free Internet account thanks to your school, remember that the institution is paying for that connection and funding it in part from your tuition. If your workplace offers Internet access and doesn't limit your use of it, consider that a benefit of working there, along with retirement and health benefits. And an increasingly large number of people, like me, pay directly, usually somewhere between $5 and $30 per month. Sure beats cable television.

Remember how I previously said that the NSFNET was created to carry supercomputer traffic but soon found itself being used for all sorts of tasks? That's another basic principle to keep in mind about how the Internet is funded. The network links were created for a specific reason (supercomputer access), and because of that reason, the money necessary to create and maintain those links was allocated in various budgets. Thus, when traffic unrelated to the supercomputer access travels on the same network, it's piggy-backing on the lines that have already been paid for out of existing budgets. So it seems free, and as long as the ancillary traffic doesn't impinge on the supercomputer access, no one is likely to complain. It's much like using your friend's computer's processing power to generate processor-intensive pictures when he's not using it. As long as your use doesn't slow down the things he wants to do, he probably won't mind, especially if it helps you finish your work sooner. But, if your use prevents him from doing his own work, he'll probably become less generous about it.

So, if the Internet did indeed move from governmental to private control, most people would not see the difference because their organizations would continue to foot the bill, especially if the costs didn't change. The danger is to poorly funded organizations such as grade schools and public libraries, which may only be able to afford their Internet connections with help from the government. Oh, and where do you think the government gets the money? Taxes, of course. So you end up paying one way or another.

Politics

After all of this discussion, you're probably confused as to who runs what on the Internet. Good, that's the way it should be, because no one person or organization runs the Internet as such. I think of the Internet as a collection of fiefdoms that must cooperate to survive. The fiefdoms are often inclusive as well, so one group may control an entire network, but another group controls a specific machine in that network. You as a user must abide by what both of them say, or find another host.

I don't mean to say that there aren't some guiding forces. The NSF exercised a certain influence over much of the Internet because it controlled a large part of it in the NSFNET. Thus, the NSF's Acceptable Use Policies (which state that the NSFNET may not be used for "commercial activities") became important rules to follow, or at least keep in mind, and I'll bet that many commercial providers used them as a starting point for creating their own less restrictive, acceptable use policies.

Several other important groups exist, all of which are volunteer-based (as is most everything on the Internet). The Internet Architecture Board, or IAB, sets the standards for the Internet. Without standards the Internet wouldn't be possible, because so many types of hardware and software exist on it. Although you must be invited to be on the IAB, anyone can attend the regular meetings of the Internet Engineering Task Force, or IETF. The IETF's meetings serve as a forum to discuss and address the immediate issues that face the Internet as a whole. Serious problems, or rather problems that interest a sufficient number of volunteers, result in working groups that report back to the IETF with a recommendation for solving the problem. This system seems haphazard, but frankly, it works, which is more than you can say for certain other organizations we could probably name.

Other networks undoubtedly have their controlling boards as well, but the most interesting is Usenet, which has even less organization than the Internet as a whole. Due to its roots in the user community, Usenet is run primarily by the community, as strange as that may sound. Every network administrator controls what news can come into her machine but can't control what goes around her machine. The converse applies as well—if a sufficient number of network administrators don't approve of something, say a newsgroup creation, then it simply doesn't happen. Major events on Usenet must have sufficient support from a sufficient number of people.

Of course, some people's votes count more than others. These people are sometimes called *net heavies* because they often administer major sites or run important mailing lists. The net heavies consider it their job (who knows how they manage to keep real jobs with all the work they do here) to keep the nets running smoothly. Even though they often work behind the scenes, they do an excellent job. Shortly after I started *TidBITS*, for instance, I was searching for the best ways to distribute it. I wasn't able to run a mailing list from my account at Cornell, and *TidBITS* was too big to post to a general Usenet group every week. After I spoke with several of the net heavies, they allowed me to post to a moderated newsgroup, `comp.sys.mac.digest`, that had up to that point been used only for distributing the Info-Mac Digest to Usenet.

If you want to get involved with what organization there is on the Internet, I suggest that you participate and contribute to discussions about the future of the nets. Gradually, you'll learn how the system works and find yourself in a position where you can help the net continue to thrive.

You should keep one thing in mind about the Internet and its loose controlling structure: It works, and it works far better than do most other organizations. By bringing control down to almost the individual level but by requiring cooperation to exist, the Internet works without the strong central government that most countries use and claim is necessary to avoid lawlessness and anarchy. Hmm...

The Internet makes you think, and that's good.

The Future

I hope this section has provided a coherent view of where the Internet has come from, along with some of the people and networks that were instrumental in its growth. After any history lesson, the immediate question concerns the future. Where can we expect the Internet to go from here?

Part IV

I'm an optimist. I'm sure you can find someone more than happy to tell you all the horrible problems—technical, political, and social—facing the Internet. I don't hold with such attitudes, though, because something that affects so many people around the world didn't appear so quickly for no reason. In one way or another, I think most people understand on a visceral level that the Internet is good, the Internet is here to stay, and if they want to be someone, they would do well to get access today and contribute in a positive fashion. Of course, books like this one only encourage such utopian attitudes.

In any event, I predict that the Internet will continue growing at an incredible rate. You might make an argument for the rate of growth slowing from its 15 percent per month rate based on the fact that it's silly to assume that anything can continue to grow at such a breakneck speed. A naysayer also might point at the massive influx of novices as endangering the Internet, or point at the increased level of commercialization as a major problem. I feel that such growth is self-propelling and that bringing more people and resources onto the Internet only further fuels the expansion. I think that growth is good—the more people, the more resources, the more opinions, the better off we all are.

I also expect to see the Internet continue to standardize, both officially and informally. At lower levels, more computers will start to use IP instead of BITNET's NJE or the aging UUCP protocols. It's merely a matter of keeping up with the Joneses, and the Joneses are running IP. At a higher level, I think that using various network resources will become easier as they start migrating toward similar interfaces. Just as it's easy to use multiple applications because you always know how to open, close, save, and quit, so it will be easier to use new and enhanced services on the Internet because they will resemble each other more and more. Even now, people rely heavily on network conventions such as prefixing site names to indicate what services they provide, like `ftp.tidbits.com` for FTP, `gopher.seattle.wa.us` for Gopher, and `www.wired.com` for the World-Wide Web.

And yes, I fully expect to see the Internet become more and more commercial, both in terms of where the service comes from and in terms of the traffic the Internet carries. However, we must remember the old attitudes about commercial use of the Internet. In the past, commercial use was often acceptable if it wasn't blatant, was appropriately directed, and was of significant value to the readers. In other words, I'll be as angry as the next person if I start receiving automatically generated junk email every day, just as I receive junk mail via snail mail. If such things start happening, the course of action will be the same as it always has been: politely ask the originator to stop once, and then, if that doesn't work, flame away—that is, send back an outrageously nasty message.

Even though I'm optimistic, I know that problems will occur. For example, consider the so-called Green Card debacle. In the spring of 1994, the husband and wife law firm of Canter & Siegel posted a blatantly commercial message advertising a green card lottery and immigration services. That wasn't the problem. The problem was that they posted it to all 5,000 Usenet newsgroups, an act called *spamming*. Discussions about Celtic culture, Macintosh communications (where I first saw it), and Washington state politics were all interrupted, along with thousands of others completely apathetic about anything to do with immigration. Or at least they were apathetic until they were bludgeoned repeatedly with Canter & Siegel's post. All of a sudden everyone cared a great deal about immigration and sent 30,000 flame messages to the offenders. That many messages was far more than Canter & Siegel's provider, Internet Direct, could handle, and their machine went down like a boxer on the wrong end of a knock-out punch.

The aftershocks keep coming, with Internet Direct suing Canter & Siegel for violating acceptable use policies (it seems that Canter & Siegel never signed the terms and conditions form) and for the detrimental effect the post had on business. In return Canter & Siegel counter-sued for loss of business, claiming some ludicrous percentage of the messages were requests for more information (though they refused to provide any verifiable data). Needless to say, Internet Direct disabled their account immediately, and details about Canter & Siegel's history began to surface. They'd been kicked off of other providers for similar smaller-scale posts in the past, they'd been suspended from the bar in Florida in 1987 for conduct the Supreme Court of Florida deemed "contrary to honest," and so on. Canter & Siegel garnered a huge amount of press (most of it negative, but as the saying goes, "I don't care what you say about me as long as you spell my name right."). They even announced in a newspaper interview that they were setting up a company to provide services to other companies who wanted to flood Usenet with advertising, and that they were going to write a book about how to advertise on the Internet. That's a bit like serial cannibal Jeffrey Dahmer writing a book about preserving meat.

The Canter & Siegel fiasco raises the question of how the Internet should be policed. In the past and the present, any transgression has been dealt with much as it might have been in the perhaps-fictional view of the American Old West. Everyone takes justice into his own hands, and if a few innocents are hurt in the process, well, it was for the greater good. When Canter & Siegel spammed Usenet, thousands of people spammed them back.

This process is more commonly known as *mail bombing*. Mail bombs are generally small UNIX programs that simply send a user-configured number of messages (using a specified file as the message body) to a given address, potentially ensuring that none of the mail bomb messages come from real addresses. A better solution came from a Norwegian programmer, who created a spambot (his term, not mine) program that somehow figures out which newsgroups Canter & Siegel spammed (yes, it happened again, although on a smaller scale) and bounces the spamming message back to them, along with a short note daring them to sue him, since he's in Norway.

Frontier justice sounds like great fun, especially when slimy lawyers are on the other end, but it raises some interesting issues. Mail bombing a machine doesn't affect just that machine—it affects many of the machines nearby on the Internet. In the case of a public machine like Internet Direct's `indirect.com`, it also hurts an innocent business and hundreds of innocent users who also use that machine. And, although the Internet as a whole can deal with the occasional mail bomb attack, if such things happened every day, they would seriously impair Internet communications. Such possibilities raise the specter of regulation, something that most Internet users disapprove of (though certain usage regulations are built into the service agreements of almost every Internet provider for liability reasons). So, will the government get involved and lay down the law about inappropriate Internet use? Probably not. The people who must do the regulation are the providers themselves—there's no way to prevent everyone from retaliating from such spam attacks as Canter & Siegel's, so the best place to stop them is at the level of the providers. They can simply refuse to give problem users an account or remove accounts when abuse occurs. But the government itself? I certainly hope not.

I don't believe that the Internet will ever be governed to a much greater extent than it now is (at least in the U.S.), simply because I don't believe it's feasible. How can you govern something that spans the globe or police something that carries gigabytes of data every day? The U.S. government could easily ban pornographic postings, say, but how does that affect someone from a different country? Or how does that affect U.S. users retrieving the pornographic images from another country? Remember, the Internet can just route around censorship. It's all very confusing, and it will be some time (if ever) before the government understands all of the issues surrounding the Internet sufficiently to produce reasonable legislation. Of course, that begs the question of unreasonable legislation, but that's always a fear.

The way the government as a whole currently views the Internet reminds me a bit of the joke about how to tell if you have an elephant in your fridge. The answer is by the footprints in the peanut butter—it's the middle of the night, and the government is standing at the open door, yawning and blinking at those massive footprints. Luckily, different parts of the government are starting to wake up, which should help dispel the dangerous ignorance that has marked certain past government Internet actions. For example, there was the Steve Jackson case, in which the CIA completely inappropriately confiscated the computer systems of a popular publisher of role-playing games. The damage award from that case enabled Steve Jackson Games to create an Internet provider called Illuminati Online (`io.com`). Perhaps the greater problem now with the government's view of the Internet is that it seems more concerned with regulating occasional outrageous behavior than with using the power of the Internet to further the public good. Personally, I prefer my government to be more interested in helping than in regulating. Of course, then there are the people who would prefer that the government just stayed out of the way, but somehow I doubt that will happen any time soon.

Index

A

Acceptable Use Policies (NSFNET), 86
access method (providers), 46
addresses of providers, 46
AIDS (ColumbiaNet), 16
all things NYC (local information sites), 36
announcements (local information sites), 35
Archie, 66-68
  Bunyip Information Systems, 67
  servers, 67-68
ARPA (Advanced Research Projects Agency), 72-75
ARPAnet (Advanced Research Projects Agency Network), 73
arts/culture sites
  museums, 41
  SOHO art scene, 18
  theaters, 42-43

B

bars and pubs (night life sites), 39
baseball sites
  Mets, 12, 29-30
  Yankees, 12, 30
basketball sites (Knicks), 13, 30-31
Bills site (football), 14, 31
BITNET, 77
  CREN, 79
  CSNET (Computer and Science Network), 80
  Freeman, Gleydon, 79
  Fuchs, Ira, 79
bookstores (hobby sites), 37, 39
Branch Information Services Electronic Mall (reference site), 20
Brand, Stewart
  Cybernetic Frontiers (italic), 75
  Whole Earth Catalog, 74
browsing, 61
Bunyip Information Systems (Archie), 67

C

city facts (reference sites), 40
city news site, 15
CLIO (Cold Spring Harbor Laboratory) (reference site), 27-28
clubs (night life sites), 40
college sites
　Columbia University Web, 24
　ColumbiaNet, 16
　CUNY (City of New York University), 19, 38
　NYU (New York University), 16
Columbia University Web (reference sites), 24
ColumbiaNet (college site), 16
commercialization of Internet, 83
computer sites, 19
Connection-Machine server (WAIS), 69
costs of Internet, 82-86
CREN (BITNET), 79
CSNET (Computer and Science Network), 80
CUNY (City of New York University), 19, 38
Cybernetic Frontiers **(Brand, Stewart), 75**

D

DARPA (Defense Advanced Research Projects Agency), 74
domains (providers), 47
Dorsai (provider), 47-48

E

Echo (provider), 48
ECHO server (local information site), 17
Email, 60
　mailing lists, 62
　mailservers, 63
　snail mail, 62
Explore New York (local information sites), 20

F

feeds (USENET), 78
File Transfer Protocol (FTP), 65-66
fileservers (Email), 63
football sites
　Bills, 14, 31
　Giants, 13, 32
　Jets, 14, 32-33
for sale (local information sites), 33-34
Freeman, Gleydon (BITNET), 79
French (reference sites), 42

Index

ftp (File Transfer Protocol), 6, 65-66
  Archie, 66-68
  servers, 47-54
Fuchs, Ira (BITNET), 79
future of the Internet, 88-94

G

gateways, 76-94
Giants site (football), 13, 32
Gopher, 6, 69
  Jughead, 70
  Veronica, 70
Gore, Al (NREN), 81-82
government regulation of Internet, 93
Green Card debacle, 90
guest accounts (providers), 47

H

hobby sites
  bookstores, 37, 39
  Nero Ashbury roleplaying, 29
  Sound Advice (music), 28
hockey sites (Rangers), 14
host machines, 59
hotels (reference sites), 41
http (HyperText Transfer Protocol), 6
hypertextual links (WWW), 71

I

IETF (Internet Engineering Task Force), 87
Internet, 58-61
  ARPA (Advanced Research Projects Agency), 72-75
  ARPAnet (Advanced Research Projects Agency Network, 73
  BITNET, 77, 79-80
  browsing, 61
  commercialization, 83
  costs, 82-86
  DARPA (Defense Advanced Research Projects Agency), 74
  future, 88-94
  gateways, 76-94
  government regulation, 93
  Green Card debacle, 90
  growth, 89
  host machines, 59
  IETF (Internet Engineering Task Force), 87
  JANET, 77
  Licklider, J.C.R., 73
  Milnet (Military Network), 76
  net heavies, 87
  NREN (National Research and Education Network), 81-82
  NSFNET (National Science Foundation Network), 80
  Acceptable Use Policies, 86
  regulations, 87
  Roberts, Larry, 74

97

Internet New York

searching, 61
Sutherland, Ivan, 73
TAP (Taxpayer Assets
   Project), 84
Taylor, Robert, 73
usage-based pricing, 84
USENET, 77-78
Whole Earth Catalog, The,
   74
Internet Relay Chat, 60

J-K

JANET, 77
**Jets site (football), 14,
   32-33**
Jughead, 70
**JvNCnet (national
   provider), 51-52**

**Knicks site (basketball),
   13, 30-31**

L

Licklider, J.C.R., 73
**local information sites,
   15**
   all things NYC, 36
   announcements, 35
   city news, 15
   ECHO server, 17
   Explore New York, 20
   for sale, 33-34
   political discussions, 34
   seminars, 34, 36
   upstate New York, 11-12
   Web browser, 21-23

M

**Maestro (provider),
   48-49**
mail bombing, 92
mailing lists (Email), 62
mailservers (Email), 63
**membership on the
   Internet, 89**
**Mets site (baseball), 12,
   29-30**
**Milnet (Military
   Network), 76**
**MindVox (provider),
   49-50**
mirror sites (FTP), 66
**MUDs (Multi-User
   Dungeons), 60, 72**
**museums (art/culture
   sites), 41**
**music sites (Sound
   Advice), 28**

N

national providers
   JvNCnet, 51-52
   Netcom, 52-53
   PSI, 53-54
**Nero Ashbury
   roleplaying (hobby
   site), 29**
net heavies, 87
**Netcom (national
   provider), 52-53**
**New York information
   (reference site), 37**
**New York Public
   Library (reference
   site), 36**

Index

night life sites
  bars and pubs, 39
  clubs, 40
NREN (National Research and Education Network), 81-82
NSFNET (National Science Foundation Network)
  Acceptable Use Policies, 86
  Internet, 80
NYC food (restaurant sites), 35
NYC Information Page (reference sites), 25-26
NYU (New York University) site, 16

P

Panix (provider), 50
Pipeline (provider), 50-51
political discussions (local information site), 34
protocols
  BITNET, 77
  JANET, 77
providers, 46
  Dorsai, 47-48
  Echo, 48
  Maestro, 48-49
  MindVox, 49-50
  national
    JvNCnet, 51-52
    Netcom, 52-53
    PSI, 53-54
  Panix, 50

Pipeline, 50-51
PSI (national provider), 53-54
public access (providers), 46
Public Library of New York (reference sites), 36

R

Rangers site (hockey), 14
reference sites
  Branch Information Services Electronic Mall, 20
  city facts, 40
  CLIO (Cold Spring Harbor Laboratory), 27-28
  Columbia University Web, 24
  French, 42
  hotels, 41
  New York information, 37
  NYC Information Page, 25-26
  Public Library, 36
  subways, 26-27
  WWW servers, 23
regulations on the Internet, 87
restaurant sites, 18
  NYC food, 35
  vegetarian, 33
Roberts, Larry (Internet), 74
roleplaying (Nero Ashbury) (hobby site), 29

S

searching, 61
seminars (local information sites), 34, 36
servers
  Archie, 67-68
  FTP (File Transfer Protocol), 47-54
services areas (providers), 46
sites
  arts/culture
    museums, 41
    SOHO art scene, 18
    theaters, 42-43
  colleges
    Columbia University Web, 24
    ColumbiaNet, 16
    CUNY (City of New York University), 19, 38
    NYU (New York University), 16
  computers, 19
  hobbies
    bookstores, 37, 39
    Nero Ashbury roleplaying, 29
    Sound Advice (music), 28
  local information, 15
    all things NYC, 36
    announcements, 35
    city news, 15
    Columbia University Web, 24
    ECHO server, 17
    Explore New York, 20
    for sale, 33-34
    political discussions, 34
    seminars, 34, 36
    upstate New York, 11-12
    Web browser, 21-23
  music, Sound Advice, 28
  night life
    bars and pubs, 39
    clubs, 40
  reference
    Branch Information Services Electronic Mall, 20
    city facts, 40
    CLIO (Cold Spring Harbor Laboratory), 27-28
    French, 42
    hotels, 41
    New York information, 37
    NYC Information Page, 25-26
    Public Library, 36
    subways, 26-27
    WWW servers, 23
  restaurants, 18
    NYC food, 35
    vegetarian, 33
  sports
    Bills, 14, 31
    Giants, 13, 32
    Jets, 14, 32-33
    Knicks, 13, 30-31
    Mets, 12, 29-30
    Rangers, 14
    Yankees, 12, 30
snail mail, 62
SOHO art scene (arts/culture site), 18
Sound Advice (music site), 28
spambots, 92
spamming
  mail bombing, 92
  Internet, 91

Index

sports sites
  baseball
    Mets, 12, 29-30
    Yankees, 12, 30
  basketball (Knicks), 13, 30-31
  football
    Bills, 14, 31
    Giants, 13, 32
    Jets, 14, 32-33
  hockey (Rangers), 14
subways (reference site), 26-27
supercomputers (NSFNET), 80
Sutherland, Ivan, 73

T

TAP (Taxpayer Assets Project), 84
Taylor, Robert, 73
TCP/IP (USENET), 78
Telnet, 65
theaters (art/culture sites), 42-43

U

upstate New York site, 11-12
URLs (Uniform Resource Locators), 5-7
usage-based pricing (Internet), 84
USENET, 60, 77-78
  feeds, 78
  TCP/IP, 78
Usenet News, 64-65

V

vegetarian restaurant sites, 33
Veronica, 70

W

WAIS (Wide Area Information Server), 6, 68
  Connection-Machine server, 69
Web browser (local information site), 21-23
***Whole Earth Catalog, The* (Brand, Stewart), 74**
WWW (World-Wide Web), 47, 71
  http (HyperText Transfer Protocol), 6
  hypertextual links, 71
WWW servers (reference site), 23

X-Y-Z

Yankees site (baseball), 12, 30